Visualize
World Geography
In 7 Minutes a Day

Let Pictography
Take you from
Clueless
to Knowing
the World

written and illustrated by

Theresa A. Blain

Tender Heart Press

Cover design by David Sean Stringer @ Mid-Cities Community Church

So that in all things God may be glorifed through Jesus Christ, to whom belong the glory and the dominion forever and ever (1Peter 4:11).

Acknowledgments

I would like to give a special thanks to my husband, Gregg, who is simply the best. Thanks for taking wonderful care of our two children, Hunter and Gregory, while I was glued to the computer, and for forever being my bud.

I would like to thank my father, Alex Saldana, for exemplifying a "never say die" attitude, and for teaching me the importance of sportsmanship. I would like to thank my mother, Theresa Lewis, for your love, and for being the hardest working person I know.

Thanks to my sisters Josie Rodriguez, Ana Maria Saldana-Furseth, and Jill Bednarz who I call on to share in every baby step I take. Also, I would like to acknowledge the fact that it is only because of Josie Rodriguez's initial collaboration on the illustrations, that I was able to take them to their present form. Thanks to my beautiful daughter, Sophia Sabey, for your help at the library in Chicago.

I would like to acknowledge Kathryn Graybill, for your many suggestions, particularly the "color flag" activity. Thanks to authors, Coni and Don Aldridge, for being inspiring role models. Thank you Rachel Harmon, Elementary Principal, and Michele Moskos, Marketing Director, of Texas Tech University Outreach and Extended Studies, for planting the seeds of this project.

Thank you Pastor Kevin York for your leadership and encouragement, and for being the instrument to awaken the call on my life.

Thank you David Sean Stringer for glorifying our Lord through your creative genius.

Thanks to Pastor Jerry Carter and Carolyn Sanders for your prayers.

Thanks to Pastor Rice Broocks for your book, *Every Nation in Our Generation,* which spoke directly to my spirit, and was the catalyst for putting *Visualize World Geography* into its present format.

PREFACE

Dear Students;

Learning about geography has now been made painless and practically effortless via Pictography! Pictography takes what the scientific community knows about <u>effective</u> memory encoding/retrieval processes in our brains, and strategically applies it to your learning of geography. This strategy mainly consists of integrating factual "geo info" (geographical information) with creative visual input, and predetermined storyline associations (labeled as mnemonic devices).

These mnemonic devices are derived from the fact that "elaborative encoding" processes ensure significantly higher retrieval success than does encoding new information only superficially.*1 In other words, the more associations you begin to use to connect incoming geo info with easy, everyday words, like clown, eagle, chili pepper, etc., the more successful you will be in remembering this new geo info. Moreover, when you take all these associations, and <u>organize</u> them by putting them is a story, or visually (pictography) or in auditory form (music jingles), or combining all of the above formats, you are sure to be a success at geography!

Neuroscientists, with nothing better to do, have devised ways of peering into the heads of volunteers, e.g., PET scans and functional MRI techniques, while these volunteers engage in "elaborative encoding" activities to learn which brain regions are involved.

*1 Gary L. Bradshaw and John R. Anderson, "Elaborative Encoding as an Explanation of Levels of Processing," <u>Journal of Verbal Learning and Verbal Behavior</u> v.21 (1982) 165-174.

Can you believe that researchers actually sit around and subtract the estimated blood flow during nonelaborative tasks from the estimated blood flow during elaborative tasks just to point to the left inferior prefrontal cortex of the brain, and say, "Yep, this part right here along with the hippocampus is real important in elaborative encoding"?

In addition, some researchers at Carnegie Mellon University wondered if average students could be trained to have superior memory skills. They recruited two average undergraduate students to make weekly vigils to the psychology lab. There these students were bombarded with randomly generated strings of numbers, and asked to repeat back as many of them as they could. After about three weeks of this, one student bailed. The other one known as SF, stayed with it, even though his memory span was average (7 plus or minus 2). Then somewhere into it, SF must have thought to himself, "since I am going to be here anyway, how can I make this interesting?" That is when he decided to take a sequence of random numbers, and pretend they were related to running times, since SF liked to run track. Now SF was using this "elaborative encoding" method to remember. The outcome of this: our average SF could not just recall 7 numbers plus or minus 2, but instead, he could recall 80 numbers after just one exposure!!*2 How cool is that?

One thing more that I would like to mention is how these particular mnemonic devices have impacted me personally. I learned about cognitive processes, like memory storage, while receiving my Masters Degree from the University of Chicago. Because of my understanding of these processes, I was able to teach my children, when they

---

*2 Daniel L. Schacter, <u>Searching For Memory</u> (New York: Basic Books, 1996), p. 48.

were very young, to recognize the flag and geographic location of over 185 nations. Since it is still somewhat unusual that a three year old has this type of geographic knowledge, my son, Hunter, was invited to several national talk shows, as well as being recognized by the Texas State Legislature.*3 The point being: if a three year old can do it, so can you!!!

Here's how it works. Start with a pictography. For a day's study, pick only one or two of the nations found within the pictography. Identify the part of the pictography depicted by each nation, e.g., eagle's head is Egypt. Ask yourself: What is the name of the eagle's head? It's Egypt. Listen to the CD for correct pronunciation of nation's name and capital city and/or jingle.

Next, look at the flag of each nation. Say the nation and capital over and over to yourself while recreating its flag either in the book, or on a separate sheet of paper--older students use colored pencils, while younger students use crayons.

Later in the day look at the particular pictography's flag section. For example, the "Eagle on Rock" flag section is found on page 24. Look for the one or two flags that you are learning for that day. Identify them by pointing at each and reciting their names. Also, ask yourself that nation's capital while pointing to its flag. (This task takes about 30 seconds).

Another task that takes about 30 seconds is to look back at the complete pictography. Throughout the day, point to the nations you are learning, and simply identify them. If you do not happen to have

*3 Regis and Kathie Lee Show, March 1999
   The Tonight Show with Jay Leno, September 1999
   Regis and Kathie Lee Show, February 2000
   State of Texas House of Representatives, House Resolution No. 74, March 5, 2001

the book in front of you, just ask yourself for example, what is the name of the eagle's head? Answer: Egypt; capital-Cairo. It's that easy!

After learning all the nations for a particular pictography, take the quiz at the end of the section. Do not proceed to next pictography until you can identify each geographic location and flag with ease.

Now after you have learned all of the nations' flags and their geographic locations, go back through the book, and fill out each nation's name, capital, and boundaries while learning specific facts that are of interest to you. The important point is to do this for only one or two nations a day. Learning two nations a day, five days a week is optimal for fastest results. However, the main idea in all of this is to enjoy the process! Have fun with it, and God bless, as you embark on a trip around the world using pictographies.

Table of Contents

Africa
Eagle on Rock

2
Burundi

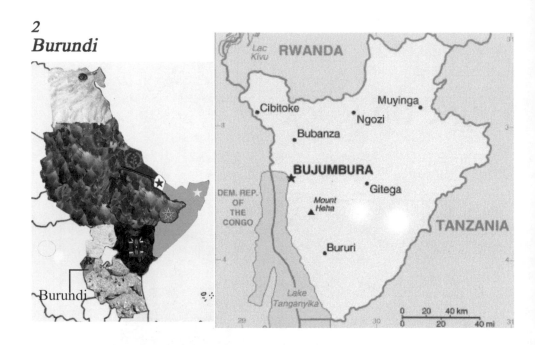

Mnemonic Device: <u>Burundi</u> is the <u>lower talon</u> of our Eagle Pictography. Because this green talon rests on top of a very cold rock, we say Burrrrr. Since it is under the other talon, we say undi. Burrrr-undi. Fold arms and shiver.

Use Map and Fill in Facts.

Name of Nation_____
Capital_____
Boundaries (Bordering Nations and/or Bodies of Water):
1._____ 2._____3._____

4._____

Area: 10,745 sq. mi. **Comparative size:** slightly smaller than Maryland
Terrain: hilly and mountainous, dropping to a plateau in east, some plains
Climate: Temperature varies with altitude. Wet seasons are from February-May;
September-November. Dry seasons are from June to August; December-January.
Geographic note: landlocked
Population: 6,373,002 people
Languages: (official) Kirundi and French; Swahili (along Lake Tanganyika and in the
Bujumbura area)
Religion: Christian 67% (Catholic 62%; Protestant5%); Indigenous beliefs 23%;
Muslim 10%
Type of Government: Republic
Exports: coffee, tea, sugar, cotton, hides
Currency: Burundi franc (BIF)

FLAG DESCRIPTION: It is divided by a white diagonal cross into two
red panels (top and bottom) and two green panels (hoist side and fly side).
There is a white disk superimposed at the center bearing three, red, six-
pointed stars which are outlined in green. The stars are arranged in a
triangular design (one star above, two stars below).

Draw and Color Flag.

Hoist   Fly

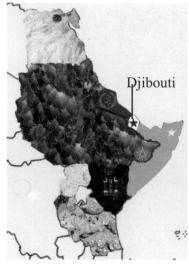

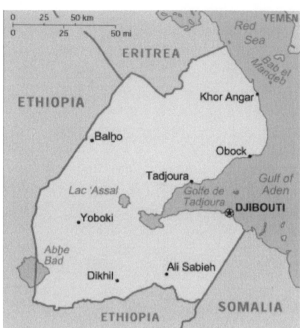

Mnemonic Device: Sung to the tune of K.C. and the Sunshine Band's "Shake Your Bootie". Replace lyrics with shake, shake, shake, shake Djibouti while shaking elbow. One's elbow corresponds to the starred-wing joint of our Eagle Pictography. This <u>starred-wing joint</u> is <u>Djibouti</u>.

Use Map and Fill in Facts.

Name of Nation_____

Capital_____

Boundaries (Bordering Nations and/or Bodies of Water):

1._____ 2._____3._____

4._____ 5._____

Area: 8,958 sq. mi. **Comparative size:** slightly smaller than Massachusetts
Terrain: coastal plain and plateau separated by central mountains
Climate: desert, torrid, dry
Geographic Note: Strategic location near world's busiest shipping lanes and close to
Arabian oilfields; terminus of rail traffic into Ethiopia, mostly wasteland
Population: 472,810 people
Languages. (official) French and Arabic; Somali, Afar
Religion: Muslim 94%, Christian 6%
Type of Government: Republic
Exports: reexports, hides and skins, coffee (in transit)
Currency: Djibouti franc (DJF)

FLAG DESCRIPTION: There are two equal horizontal bands of light
blue (top) and green with a white isosceles triangle based on the hoist side
bearing a red, five-pointed star in the center.

Draw and Color Flag.

Hoist

Fly

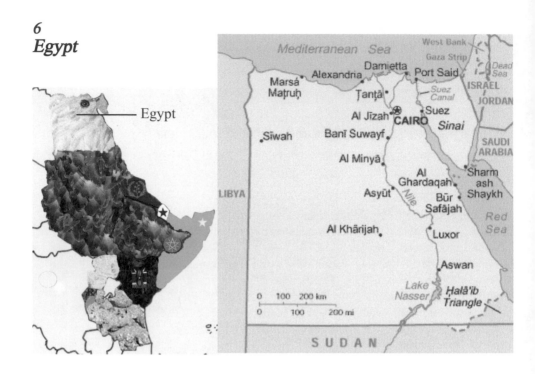

Egypt

Mnemonic Device: Egypt is the <u>head</u> of our Eagle Pictography. An eagle is the device used in Egypt's flag.

Use Map and Fill in Facts.

Name of Nation_____
Capital_____
Boundaries (Bordering Nations and/or Bodies of Water):
1._____ 2._____ 3._____
4._____ 5._____

Area:386,660 sq. mi. **Comparative size:** about three times the size of New Mexico
Terrain: vast desert plateau interrupted by Nile valley and delta
Climate: desert, hot, dry summers with moderate winters
Geographic Note: Controls Sinai Peninsula, only land bridge between Africa and
remainder of Eastern Hemisphere; controls Suez Canal, shortest sea link between Indian
Ocean and Mediterranean Sea; size, and juxtaposition to Israel, establishes it as a major
player in the geopolitics of the Middle East. It is prone to influx of refugees.
Population: 70,712,345 people
Languages: (official) Arabic; English and French widely understood by educated classes
Religion: Muslim (mostly Sunni) 94%, Coptic Christian and other 6%
Type of Government: Republic
Exports: Crude oil and petroleum products, cotton, textiles, metal products, chemicals
Currency: Egyptian pound (EGP)

FLAG DESCRIPTION: There are three equal horizontal bands of red
(top), white, and black with the national emblem (a shield superimposed on
a golden eagle facing the hoist side above a scroll bearing the name of the
country in Arabic) centered in the white band.

Draw and Color Flag.

Hoist

Fly

Eritrea

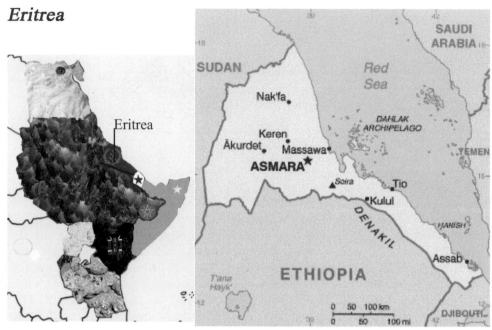

Mnemonic Device: Eritrea uses a device on its flag of an olive branch that resembles a young <u>tree</u>. To encourage its growth, we are going to cheer it on like this: Eri-<u>tree</u>-a, Eri-<u>tree</u>-a, Rah, Rah!! You can see this device on the Eagle's <u>top wing</u> which is the geographic location of <u>Eritrea</u>.

Use Map and Fill in Facts.

Name of Nation_____
Capital_____
Boundaries (Bordering Nations and/or Bodies of Water):
1._____ 2._____ 3._____
4._____

Area: 46,841 sq. mi. **Comparative size:** slightly larger than Pennsylvania
Terrain: descending on the east to a coastal desert plain, on the northwest to hilly terrain and on the southwest-- flat-to-rolling plains
Climate: hot, dry desert strip along Red Sea coast; cooler and wetter in the central highlands; semiarid in western hills and lowlands; rainfall heaviest during June-September except in coastal desert
Geographic Note: Strategic geopolitcal position along world's busiest shipping lanes; Eritrea retained the entire coastline of Ethiopia along the Red Sea upon independence from Ethiopia.
Population: 4,465,651 people
Languages: Afar, Amharic, Arabic, Tigre and Kunama, Tigrinya
Religion: Muslim, Coptic Christian, Roman Catholic, Protestant
Type of Government: Transitional government
Exports: livestock, sorghum, textiles, food, small manufactures
Currency: nakfa (ERN)

FLAG DESCRIPTION: There is a red isosceles triangle (based on the hoist side) dividing the flag into two right triangles; the upper triangle is green, the lower one is blue. A gold wreath encircling a gold olive branch is centered on the hoist side of the red triangle.

Draw and Color Flag.

Hoist

Fly

Ethiopia

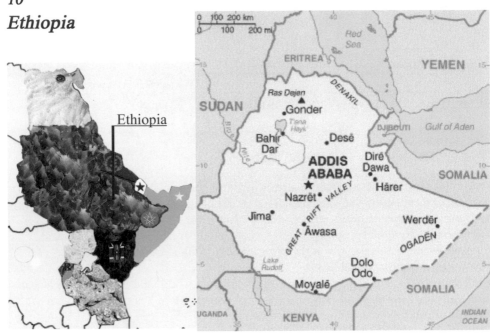

Ethiopia

Mnemonic Device: Imagine you are soaring on the wing of an Eagle eating tapioca. Listen to jingle on CD "Eating Tapioca on Ethiopia". Our Eagle Pictography has on its wing, the device used in Ethiopia's flag. <u>Ethiopia</u> is the large <u>wing</u> of our Eagle Pictography.

Use Map and Fill in Facts.

Name of Nation_____

Capital_____

Boundaries (Bordering Nations and/or Bodies of Water):

1._____ 2._____ 3._____

4._____ 5._____

Area: 435,186 sq. mi. **Comparative size:** slightly less than twice the size of Texas
Terrain: high plateau with central mountain range divided by Great Rift Valley
Climate: tropical monsoon with wide topographic-induced variation
Geographic Note: landlocked--entire coastline along the Red Sea was lost with Eritrea's independence on 24 May 1993.
Population: 67,673,031 people
Languages: Amharic, Tigrinya, Oromigna, Guaragigna, Somali, Arabic, English
Religion: Muslim 45 50%; Ethiopian Orthodox 35-40%; Animist 12%, other 3-8%
Type of Government: Federal Republic
Exports: coffee, qat, gold, leather products, oilseeds
Currency: birr (ETB)

FLAG DESCRIPTION: There are three equal horizontal bands of green (top), yellow, and red with a yellow pentagram and single yellow rays emanating from the angles between the points on a light blue disk centered on the three bands. Ethiopia is the oldest independent country in Africa, and the three main colors of its flag were so often adopted by other African countries upon independence, that they became know as the pan-African colors.

Draw and Color Flag.

Hoist   Fly

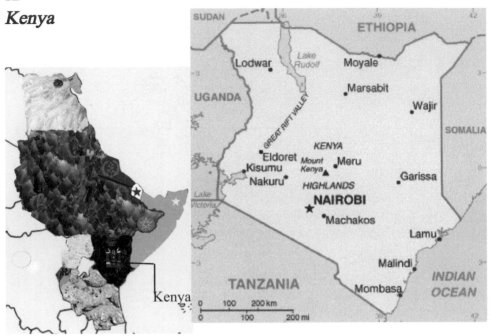

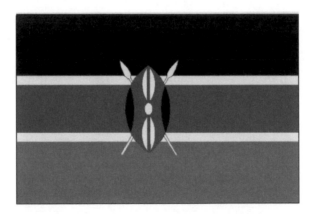

Mnemonic Device: The <u>lower body</u> of our Eagle Pictography is the nation of <u>Kenya</u>. <u>Can ya</u>, <u>can ya</u> see the device used on Kenya's flag displayed on the lower body of the eagle? <u>Can ya</u>, <u>can ya</u> huh?

Use Map and Fill in Facts.

Name of Nation_____
Capital_____
Boundaries (Bordering Nations and/or Bodies of Water):
1._____ 2._____ 3._____
4._____ 5._____ 6._____

Area: 224,960 sq. mi. **Comparative size:** about twice the size of Nevada
Terrain: low plains rise to central highlands bisected by Great Rift Valley; fertile plateau in west
Climate: Varies from tropical along coast to arid in interior
Geographic Note: Kenyan Highlands are one of the most successful agricultural production regions in Africa.
Population: 31,138,735 people
Languages: (official) English and Kiswahili, numerous indigenous languages
Religion: Protestant 45%, Roman Catholic 33%, Indigenous beliefs 10%, Muslim 10%, other 2%
Type of Government: Republic
Exports: tea, horticultural products, coffee, petroleum products, fish, cement
Currency: Kenyan shilling (KES)

FLAG DESCRIPTION: There are three equal horizontal bands of black (top), red, and green. The red band is edged in white, while a large warrior's shield covering crossed spears is superimposed at the center.

Draw and Color Flag.

Hoist

Fly

Rwanda

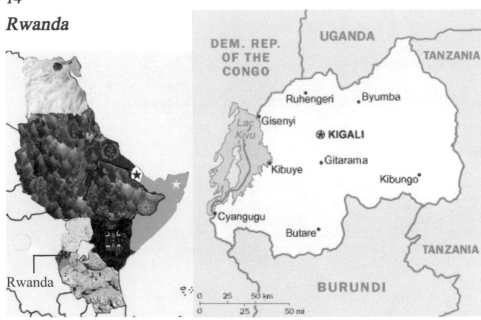

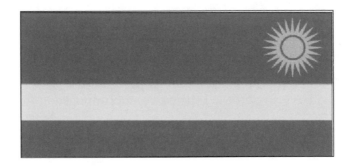

Mnemonic Device: The nation of <u>R</u>wanda is depicted as the <u>R</u>ight <u>talon</u> of our Eagle Pictography. The talon itself has an "R" on it for Right and Rwanda. Also, visualize an old, clunker of a car, and call it Wanda. Now when it is very cold outside, this car does not like to turn over very easily. Similarly, since the right talon rests on a very cold rock, we say RRRRR--Wanda (immitating the sound of an old car trying to start on a cold day).

Use Map and Fill in Facts.

Name of Nation_____

Capital_____

Boundaries (Bordering Nations and/or Bodies of Water):

1._____ 2._____ 3._____

4._____

Area: 10,169 sq. mi. **Comparative size:** slightly smaller than Maryland
Terrain: mostly grassy uplands and hills
Climate: temperate; two rainy seasons (February to April, November to January)
Geographic Note: landlocked; most of the country is savanna grassland
Population: 7,398,074 people
Languages: (official) Kinyarwanda, French, English; universal Bantu venacular
Religion: Catholic 56.5%; Protestant 26%; Adventist 11.1%; Muslim 4.6%, indigenous beliefs .1%; none 1.7%
Type of Government: Republic
Exports: coffee, tea, hides, tin ore
Currency: Rwandan franc (RWF)

FLAG DESCRIPTION: There are three horizontal bands of sky blue (top, double width), yellow, and green, with a golden sun with 24 rays near the fly end of the blue band.

Draw and Color Flag.

Hoist   Fly

Somalia

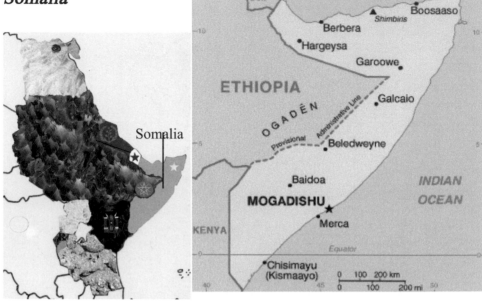

Mnemonic Device: The nation of <u>Somalia</u> is depicted as the <u>tail feathers</u> of our Eagle Pictography. These tail feathers are blanketed with blue, and display the white star as seen on Somalia's flag. Listen to Somalia's jingle on CD: "So Molly Molly... tell me Somalia."

Use Map and Fill in Facts.

Name of Nation_____
Capital_____
Boundaries (Bordering Nations and/or Bodies of Water):
1._____ 2._____3._____
4._____ 5. _____

Area: 246,200 sq. mi. **Comparative size:** slightly smaller than Texas
Terrain: mostly flat rising to hills in north
Climate: :mainly dessert; December to February- northeat monsoon; May to October-southwest monsoon; scortching hot in the north just hot in the south
Geographic Note: strategic location on the Horn of Africa
Population: 7,753,310 people
Languages: (official) Somali; Arabic, Italian, English
Religion: Sunni Muslim
Type of Government: no permanent national government; transitional
Exports: livestock, bananas, hides, fish, charcoal, scrap metal
Currency: Somali shilling (SOS)

FLAG DESCRIPTION: It has a light blue field with a large white five-pointed star in the center. The UN flag influenced the choice of the blue field.

Draw and Color Flag.

Hoist

Fly

Sudan

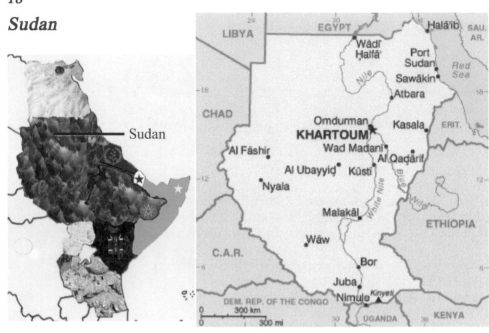

Jordan

Mnemonic Device: The nation of <u>Sudan</u> is depicted as the <u>breast</u> of our Eagle Pictography. When learning Sudan's flag, we shall also learn Jordan's flag. Listen to "Jordan, Sudan, Ol'Dan Tucker" jingle on CD.

Use Map and Fill in Facts.

Name of Nation_____
Capital_____
Boundaries (Bordering Nations and/or Bodies of Water):
1._____ 2._____ 3._____
    4._____ 5. _____
6._____7._____8._____
    9._____10._____

Area: 967,495 sq. mi. **Comparative size:** about one-quarter size of the U.S.A.
Terrain: flat, featureless plain; mountains in east and west
Climate: tropical in south; arid desert in north; rainy season from April to October
Geographic Note: largest country in Africa; dominated by the Nile and its tributaries
Population: 37,090,298 people
Languages: (official) Arabic; Nubian, Ta Bedawie, dialects of Nilotic, Nilo-Hamitic,
Sudanic, English; note: program of "Arabization" in process
Religion: Sunni Muslim 70% (in north), indigenous beliefs 25%,
Christian 5% (mostly in south and Khartoum)
Type of Government: authoritarian regime; alliance of military and National Congress
Party, which espouses an Islamist platform
Exports: oil and petroleum products, cotton, sesame, livestock, groundnuts, gum,
arabic, sugar
Currency: Sudanese dinar (SDD)

FLAG DESCRIPTION (Sudan): There are three equal horizontal bands
of red (top), white, and black with a green isosceles triangle based on the
hoist side.

Draw and Color Flag.

Hoist

Fly

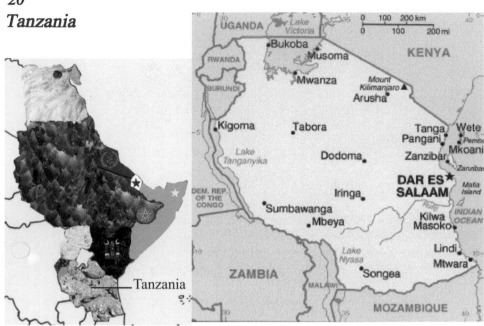

Mnemonic Device: Since Tanzania is home to Africa's highest mountain, Mt. Kilimanjaro, it is quite apropos that <u>Tanzania</u> is depicted as the cold <u>rock</u> of our Eagle Pictography. Listen to "Tanzania" jingle on CD.

Use Map and Fill in Facts.

Name of Nation_____
Capital_____
Boundaries (Bordering Nations and/or Bodies of Water):
1._____ 2._____ 3._____
4._____ 5._____ 6._____
7._____ 8._____ 9._____

Area: 364,900 sq. mi. **Comparative size:** about twice the size of California
Terrain: plains along coast; central plateau; highlands in north and south
Climate: tropical along coast; temperate in highlands
Geographic Note: Kilimanjaro is highest point in Africa; bordered by three of the
largest lakes on the continent: Lake Victoria (world's second-largest freshwater lake) in
the north, Lake Tanganyika (the world's second-deepest) in the west, and Lake Nyasa
Population: 37,187,939 people
Languages: (official) Swahili and English; Arabic, many local languages
Religion: Muslim 35%, indigenous beliefs 35%, Christian 30%
Type of Government: republic
Exports: gold, coffee, cashew nuts, manufactures, cotton
Currency: Tanzanian shilling (TZS)

FLAG DESCRIPTION (Sudan): Divided diagonally by a yellow-edged
black band from the lower hoist-side corner to the upper fly-side corner.
The upper triangle (hoist side) is green; the lower triangle (fly side) is blue.

Draw and Color Flag.

Hoist

Fly

Uganda

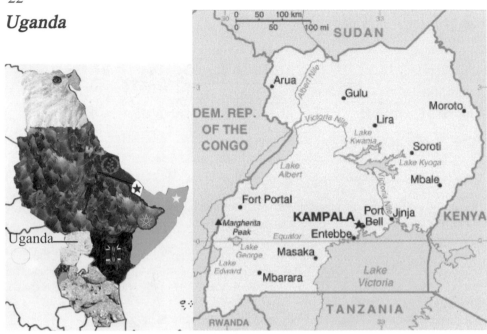

Mnemonic Device: The nation of Uganda may be pronounced
in a way that rhymes with panda. So when we view the African crane in
the center of Uganda's flag, we say it is a friend of Panda, Uganda. Also,
the long legs of the crane reminds us that <u>Uganda</u> is depicted as the yellow
<u>leg</u> of our Eagle Pictography.

Use Map and Fill in Facts.

Name of Nation_____
Capital_____
Boundaries (Bordering Nations and/or Bodies of Water):
1._____2._____3._____
4._____5._____6._____

Area: 93,104 sq. mi. **Comparative size:** slightly smaller than Oregon
Terrain: mostly plateau with rim of mountains
Climate: tropical; rainy with two dry seasons from December to February, and June to August. It is semiarid in northeast.
Geographic Note: landlocked; fertile, well-watered with many lakes and rivers
Population: 24,699,073 people
Languages: (official) English; Uganda other Niger-Congo languages, Nilo-Saharan languages, Swahili, Arabic
Religion: Catholic 33%; Protestant 33%; Indigenous beliefs 18%, Muslim 16%
Type of Government: republic
Exports:coffee, fish and fish products, tea; gold, cotton, flowers, horticultural products
Currency: Ugandan shilling (UGX)

FLAG DESCRIPTION: There are six equal horizontal bands of black (top), yellow, red, black, yellow, and red; a white disk is superimposed at the center and depicts a red-crested crane (the national symbol) facing the hoist side.

Draw and Color Flag.

Hoist   Fly

Identify Flags of Eagle Pictography.

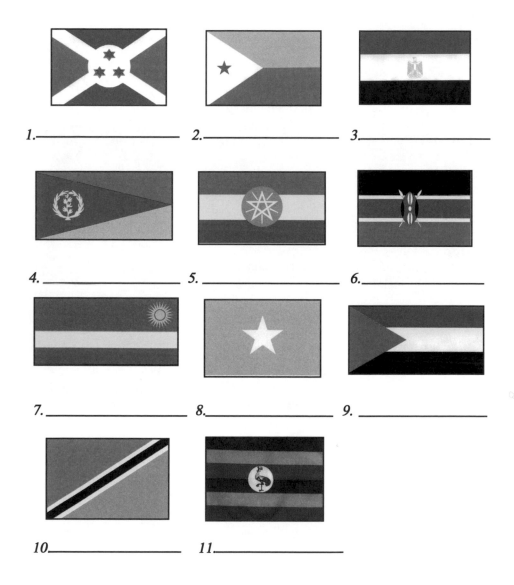

1.————————————— 2.————————————— 3.—————————————

4. ————————————— 5. ————————————— 6.—————————————

7. ————————————— 8.————————————— 9. —————————————

10.————————————— 11.—————————————

Identify Nations of Eagle Pictography.

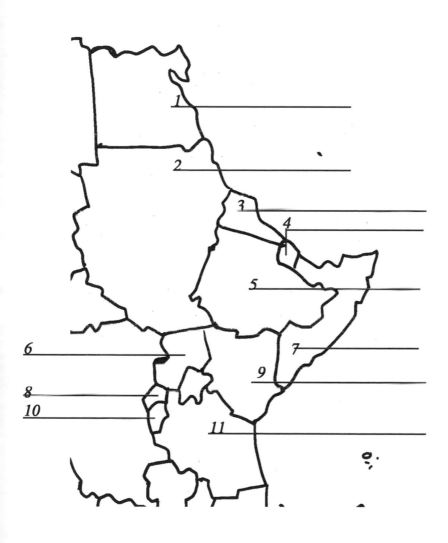

1 _____

2 _____

3 _____

4 _____

5 _____

6 _____

7 _____

8 _____

9 _____

10 _____

11 _____

Africa
Boy in Bed

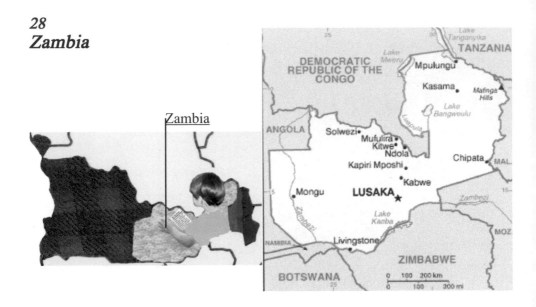

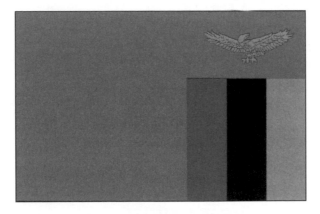

Mnemonic Device: The nation of <u>Zambia</u> is depicted as a <u>little boy</u> reading a book in bed. Now the eagle device on Zambia's flag spotted Zambia's shiny hair, and decided it would make good nesting material. So it swooped down and began to tug and pull on Zambia's hair, until it hurt little Zambia's head. After this encounter, Zambia had a headache and decided to go to bed and read a book.

Use Map and Fill in Facts.

Name of Nation_____
Capital_____
Boundaries (Bordering Nations and/or Bodies of Water):
1._____ 2._____ 3._____
4._____ 5._____ 6._____
      7._____ 8._____

Area: 290,585 sq. mi. **Comparative size:** slightly larger than Texas
Terrain: mostly high plateau with some hills and mountains
Climate: tropical; rainy season from October to April
Geographic Note: landlocked; the Zambezi forms a natural riverine boundary with Zimbabwe
Population: 9,959,037 people
Languages: (official) English; major vernaculars include Bemba, Kaonda, Lozi, Lunda, Luvale, Nyanja, Tonga; about 70 other indigenous languages
Religion: Christian 50-75%; Muslim and Hindu 24-49%; indigenous beliefs 1%
Type of Government: republic
Exports: copper 55%, cobalt, electricity, tobacco, flowers, cotton
Currency: Zambian kwacha (ZMK)

FLAG DESCRIPTION: There is a green field with a panel of three vertical bands of red, black, and orange on the hoist side. This panel is below a soaring orange eagle, displayed on the upper fly side.

Draw and Color Flag.

Hoist   Fly

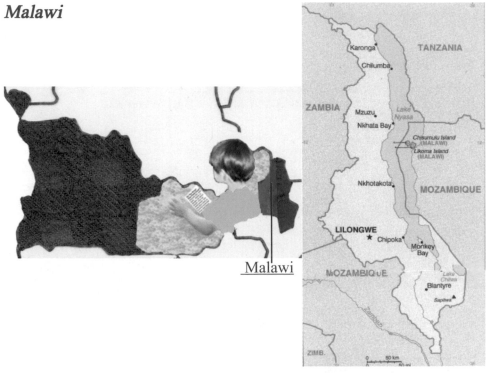

Malawi

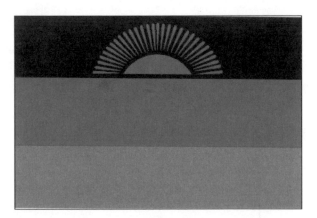

Mnemonic Device: When poor, little Zambia lays his head on his pillow, he exclaims, "Owie Malawi, owie, Malawi!!" Malawi is depicted as the pillow of our Boy in Bed Pictography.

Use Map and Fill in Facts.

Name of Nation_____
Capital_____
Boundaries (Bordering Nations and/or Bodies of Water):
1._____2._____3._____

Area: 45,747 sq. mi. **Comparative size:** slightly smaller than Pennsylvania
Terrain: elongated plateau; rolling hills, some mountains
Climate: sub-tropical; rainy season from November to May; dry season: May-November
Geographic Note: landlocked; prominent physical feature is Lake Nyasa
Population: 10,701,824 people
Languages: (official) English and Chichewa; regional languages
Religion: Protestant 55%, Catholic 20%, Muslim 20%, indigenous beliefs 3%, other 2%
Type of Government: multiparty democracy
Exports: tobacco, tea, sugar, cotton, coffee, peanuts, wood products, apparel
Currency: Malawian kwacha (NWK)

FLAG DESCRIPTION: There are three equal horizontal bands of black (top), red, and green with a radiant, rising, red sun centered in the black band.

Draw and Color Flag.

Hoist

Fly

Angola

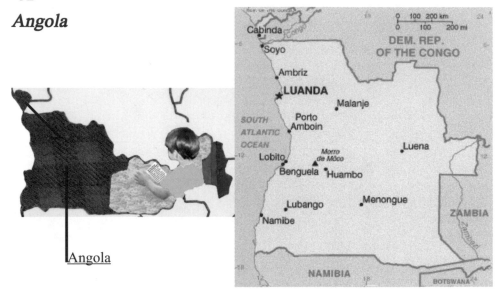

Angola

Mnemonic Device: After reading his book, Zambia desires a good night's rest. Unfortunately, the owie on the back of his head keeps him awake. Luckily, however, he owns a one-of-a-kind, singing <u>blanket</u>, named Ann. Zambia politely asks Ann to go la, la in order to be lulled asleep. Ann-go-la? Please, Ann-go-la, <u>Angola</u>.

Use Map and Fill in Facts.

Name of Nation_____
Capital_____
Boundaries (Bordering Nations and/or Bodies of Water):
1._____2._____3._____
4._____

Area: 481,351 sq. mi. **Comparative size:** a bit less than twice the size of Texas
Terrain: narrow coastal plains; vast interior plateau
Climate: semiarid in south and along Luanda's coast; north has cool, dry season from May to October, and hot, rainy season from November to April.
Geographic Note: Cabinda is separated from the rest of the country by the Democratic Republic of Congo.
Population: 10,593,171 people
Languages: (official) Portuguese; Bantu and other African languages
Religion: indigenous beliefs 47%, Catholic 38%, Protestant 15%
Type of Government: republic with strong presidential system
Exports: crude oil 90%, diamonds, refined petroleum products, gas, coffee, sisal, fish and fish products, timber, cotton
Currency: kwanza (AOA)

FLAG DESCRIPTION: There are two equal horizontal bands of red (top), and black with a centered yellow emblem. This emblem consists of a five-pointed star within half a cogwheel crossed by a machete (in the style of a hammer and sickle).

Draw and Color Flag.

Hoist

Fly

Identify Flags of Boy in Bed Pictography.

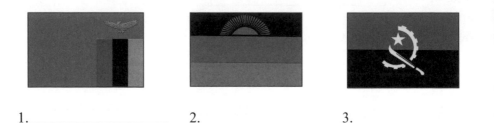

1._____   2. _____   3. _____

Identify Nations of Boy in Bed Pictography.

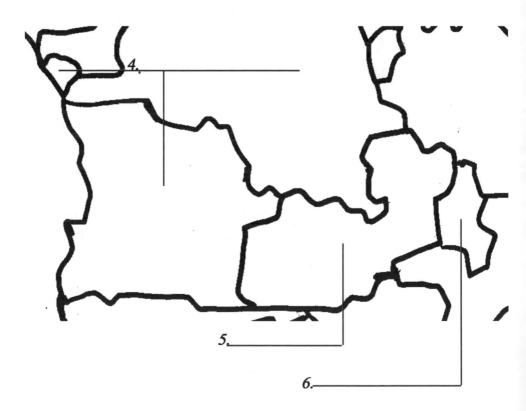

<u>Africa</u>
Poodle and Ball

Mozambique

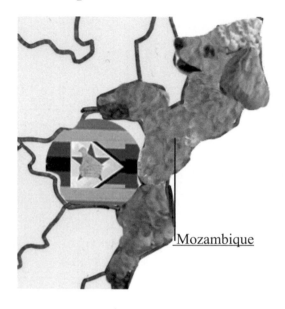

Mozambique

Mnemonic Device: Mozambique is depicted as a smart, little <u>poodle</u> standing up on his hind legs, while resting his front paws on a ball. Although he has a snout and not a beak, yet we call him, <u>Mozambique</u>.

Use Map and Fill in Facts.

Name of Nation_____

Capital_____

Boundaries (Bordering Nations and/or Bodies of Water):

1._____ 2._____ 3._____
4._____ 5._____ 6._____
7._____ 8._____

Area: 309,494 sq. mi. **Comparative size:** about twice the size of California
Terrain: mountains in the west; mostly coastal lowlands
Climate: subtropical to tropical
Geographic Note: The Zambezi river flows through the north-central and most fertile part of the country.
Population: 19,607,519 people
Languages: (official) Portuguese; indigenous dialects
Religion: indigenous beliefs 50%, Christian 30%, Muslim 20%
Type of Government: republic
Exports: prawns 40%, cashews, cotton, sugar, citrus, timber; bulk electricity
Currency: metical (MZM)

FLAG DESCRIPTION: There are three equal horizontal bands of green (top), black, and yellow with a red isosceles triangle based on the hoist side. The black band is edged in white; centered in the triangle is a yellow, five-pointed star bearing a crossed rifle and hoe in black superimposed on an open white book.

Draw and Color Flag.

Hoist

Fly

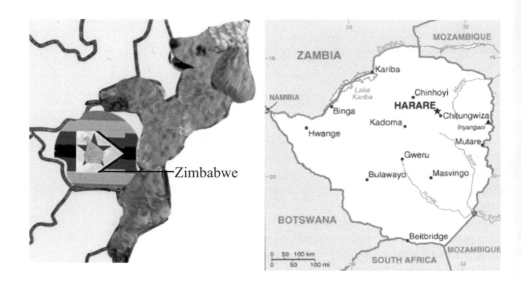

—Zimbabwe

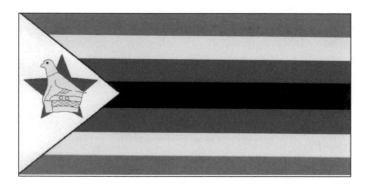

Mnemonic Device: When the poodle, Mozambique, plays with his master, Bob, the ball zooms Zis way and Zat way, <u>Zim</u>...it goes <u>Bob's way</u>. <u>Zimbabwe</u> is depicted as the <u>ball</u> in our Poodle Pictography.

Use Map and Fill in Facts.

Name of Nation_____
Capital_____
Boundaries (Bordering Nations and/or Bodies of Water):
1._____2._____3._____
4._____

Area: 150,806 sq. mi. **Comparative size:** slightly larger than Montana
Terrain: mountains in the east; mostly high plateau
Climate: tropical; rainy season from November to March
Geographic Note: Landlocked; the Zambezi river forms a natural riverine boundary
with Zambia; in full flood (February-April) Victoria Falls on the river forms the world's
largest curtain of falling water.
Population: 11,376,676 people
Languages: (official) English; Shona, Sindebele, minor tribal dialects
Religion: syncretic (part Christian, part indigenous beliefs) 50%, Christian 25%,
indigenous beliefs 24%, Muslim and other 1%
Type of Government: parliamentary democracy
Exports: tobacco 30%, gold 11%, ferroalloys 9%, textile/clothing 3%
Currency: Zimbabwean dollar (ZWD)

FLAG DESCRIPTION: There are seven equal horizontal bands of green,
yellow, red, black, red, yellow, and green with a white isosceles triangle
edged in black with its base on the hoist side. A yellow Zimbabwe bird is
superimposed on a red five-pointed star in the center of the triangle.

Draw and Color Flag.

Hoist   Fly

Identify Flags of Poodle Pictography.

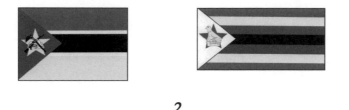

1._____   2._____

Identify Nations of Poodle Pictography.

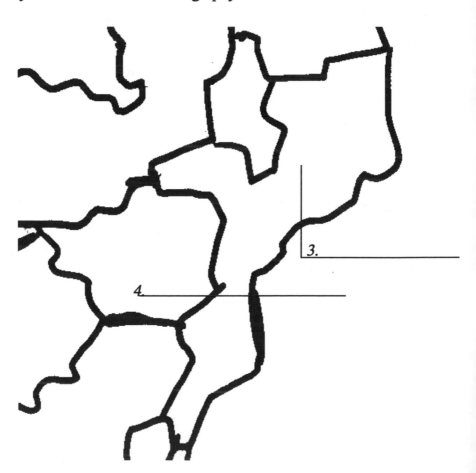

Africa
Al Cheery-A Clown

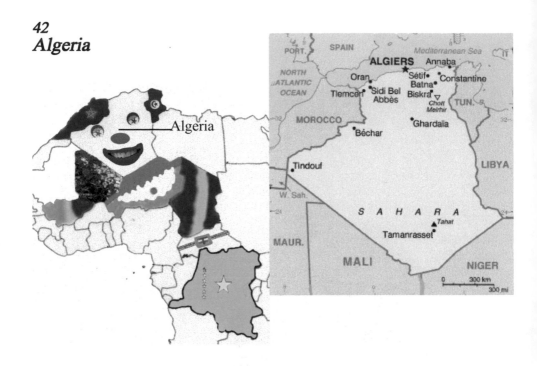

Algeria

Mnemonic Device: <u>Al Cheery-a</u> clown sounds very much like Algeria. <u>Algeria</u> is depicted as the <u>face</u> of our Clown Pictography. Al Cheery's eyes are made from the device used in Algeria's flag.

Use Map and Fill in Facts.

Name of Nation_____
Capital_____
Boundaries (Bordering Nations and/or Bodies of Water):
1._____2._____3._____
    4._____5._____
6._____7._____8._____

Area: 919,595 sq. mi. **Comparative size:** about 3 and a half times the size of Texas.
Terrain: mostly high plateau and desert; some mountains; some coastal plain
Climate: arid to semiarid; wet winters with hot, dry summers along coast; sand/dust storms common during the summer
Geographic Note: second largest country in Africa after Sudan
Population: 32,277,942 people
Languages: (official) Arabic; French, Berber dialects
Religion: Sunni Muslim (state religion) 99%, Christian and Jewish 1%
Type of Government: republic
Exports: petroleum, natural gas, and petroleum products 97%
Currency: Algerian dinar (DZD)

FLAG DESCRIPTION: There are two equal vertical bands of green (hoist side) and white (fly side). A red, five-pointed star within a red crescent centered over the two-color boundary. The crescent, star, and color green are traditional symbols of Islam (the state religion).

Draw and Color Flag.

Hoist

Fly

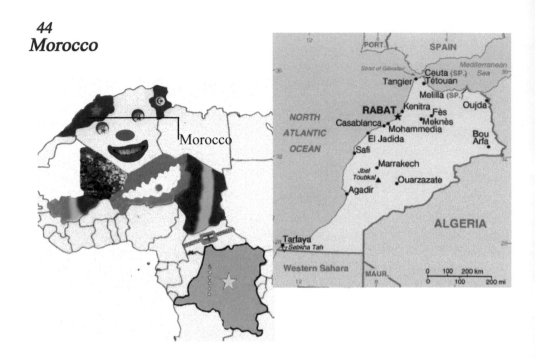

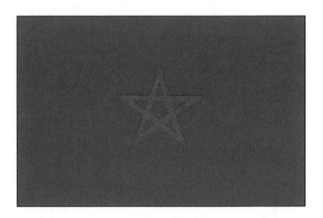

Mnemonic Device: Al Cheery uses something called "occo" in his hair to get it that fire-engine, red color. On the side of his head, where he has <u>more hair</u>, he always says, "more occo, more occo, <u>Morocco</u>, please."

Use Map and Fill in Facts.

Name of Nation_____
Capital_____
Boundaries (Bordering Nations and/or Bodies of Water):
1._____2._____3._____
   4._____5._____

Area: 157,992 sq. mi. **Comparative size:** slightly larger than California
Terrain: northern coast and interior are mountainous; rich coastal plains
Climate: Mediterranean, becoming more extreme in the interior
Geographic Note: strategic location along approach to Strait of Gibraltar
Population: 31,167,783 people
Languages: (official) Arabic; Berber dialects, French often used in diplomacy
Religion: Muslim 98.7%, Christian 1.1%, Jewish 0.2%
Type of Government: constitutional monarchy
Exports: phosphates and fertilizers, food and beverages, minerals
Currency: Moroccan dirham (MAD)

FLAG DESCRIPTION: It has a red field with a green pentacle (five-pointed, linear star) known as Solomon's seal is in the center of the flag. Green is the traditional color of Islam.

Draw and Color Flag.

Hoist   Fly

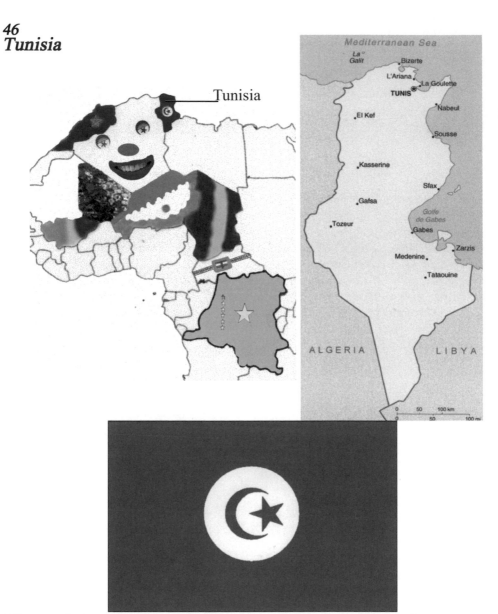

Tunisia

Mnemonic Device: The <u>other side of Al's hair</u> is fire-engine red too. In order to get it that color, we know he must rub occo into it. When Al is done rubbing occo on this side of his hair, there is always some left over. His <u>left</u> side has <u>left</u> over occo, which he then rubs on his <u>two knees</u>, <u>Tunisia.</u>

Use Map and Fill in Facts.

Name of Nation_____
Capital_____
Boundaries (Bordering Nations and/or Bodies of Water):
1._____2._____3._____

Area: 63,170 sq. mi. **Comparative size:** slightly larger than Georgia
Terrain: mountains in north; hot, dry central plain; semiarid south merges into Sahara
Climate: mild in north--rainy winters, dry summers; desert in south
Geographic Note: strategic location in central Mediterranean
Population: 9,815,644 people
Languages: (official) Arabic; French often used in commerce
Religion: Muslim 98%, Christian 1%, Jewish and other 1%
Type of Government: republic
Exports: textiles, mechanical goods, phosphates and chemicals, agricultural products, hydrocarbons
Currency: Tunisian dinar (TND)

FLAG DESCRIPTION: It has a red field with a white disk in the center. Within the white disk is a red crescent which nearly encircles a red, five-pointed star. The crescent and star are traditional symbols of Islam.

Draw and Color Flag.

Hoist

Fly

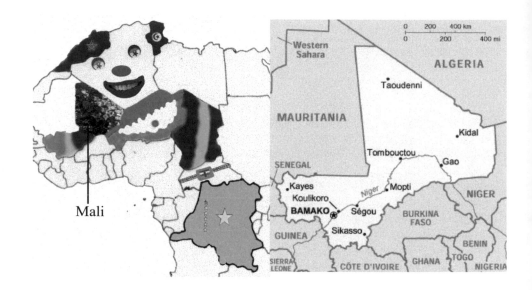

Mali

Mnemonic Device: Al Cheery is in love with a dolly, named Molly. He carries a bouquet of flowers for her. <u>Mali</u> is depicted as the <u>arm and bouquet of flowers</u> in our Clown Pictography.

Use Map and Fill in Facts.

Name of Nation_____
Capital_____
Boundaries (Bordering Nations and/or Bodies of Water):
1._____2._____3._____
    4._____5._____
    6._____7._____

Area: 465,000 sq. mi. **Comparative size:** about twice the size of Texas
Terrain: northern plains are flat to rolling covered by sand; savanna in south
Climate: subtropical to arid: hot, and dry from February to June; rainy, humid from June to November; cool and dry from November to February
Geographic Note: landlocked
Population: 11,340,480 people
Languages: (official) French, Bambara 80%; numerous African languages
Religion: Muslim 90%, indigenous beliefs 9%, Christian 1%
Type of Government: republic
Exports: cotton 43%, gold 40%, livestock
Currency: Communaute Financiere Africaine franc (XOF)

FLAG DESCRIPTION: There are three equal vertical bands: green (hoist side), yellow, and red. These are the popular pan-African colors of Ethiopia.

Draw and Color Flag.

Hoist

Fly

Mnemonic Device: <u>Niger</u> is depicted as the <u>collar</u> of our Clown Pictography. The colors and pattern of the collar are based on those of Niger's flag. When learning the flag and location of Niger, see if you can find a rhyming word for Niger.

Use Map and Fill in Facts.

Name of Nation_____

Capital_____

Boundaries (Bordering Nations and/or Bodies of Water):

1._____ 2._____ 3._____

    4._____ 5._____

    6._____ 7._____

Area: 489,000 sq. mi. **Comparative size:** about twice the size of Texas
Terrain: mainly desert plains and sand dunes; flat plains in south; hills in north
Climate: desert; mostly hot, dry, dusty; tropical in extreme south
Geographic Note: landlocked; one of the hottest countries in the world
Population: 10,639,744 people
Languages: (official) French; Hausa, Djerma
Religion: Muslim 80%, 20% indigenous beliefs and Christian
Type of Government: republic
Exports: uranium ore 65%, livestock products, cowpeas, onions
Currency: Communaute Financiere Africaine franc (XOF)

FLAG DESCRIPTION: There are three equal horizontal bands: orange (top), white, and green with a small orange disk (representing the sun) centered within the white band.

Draw and Color Flag.

Hoist

Fly

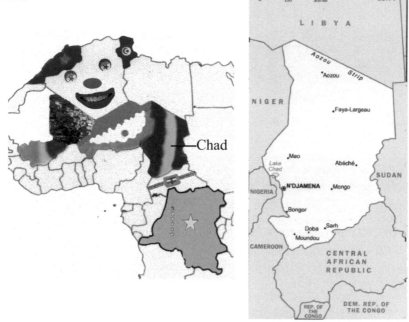

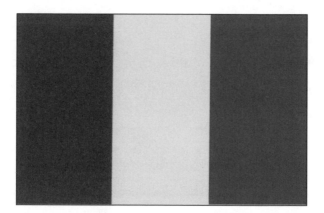

Mnemonic Device: <u>Chad</u> is depicted as Al Cheery's <u>other arm</u> which is clad in the colors of Chad's flag. Now Al had a dad, Chad, that was killed in the Arm-y. So when looking at Al Cheery's arm we chant, " had a dad, Chad, had a dad, Chad...(repeat to fade).

Use Map and Fill in Facts.

Name of Nation_____
Capital_____
Boundaries (Bordering Nations and/or Bodies of Water):
1._____ 2._____ 3._____
4._____ 5._____ 6._____

Area: 495,753 sq. mi. **Comparative size:** about three times the same as California
Terrain: desert in north, mountains in northwest, lowlands in south, plains in center
Climate:desert in north; tropical in south
Geographic Note: landlocked; Lake Chad is the most significant body of water in the Sahel
Population: 8,997,237 people
Languages: (official) French and Arabic; Sara (in south), more than 120 languages
Religion: Muslim 51%, Christian 35%, animist 7%, other 7%
Type of Government: republic
Exports: cotton, cattle, gum arabic
Currency: Communaute Financiere Africaine franc (XAF)

FLAG DESCRIPTION: Three equal vertical bands: blue (hoist side), yellow, and red. Chad's flag is like that of Romania. It is also similar to the flags of Andorra and Moldova. Each of these are designed based on the tricolored flag of France.

Draw and Color Flag.

Hoist   Fly

Central African Republic

Mnemonic Device: <u>Central African Republic</u> is depicted as the middle or <u>central</u> section of our Clown Pictography. If you look closely, you can see its flag in the buckle of Al Cheery's belt. When identifying its flag, the central, vertical stripe will prompt you to remember its name. Also, listen to CD.

Use Map and Fill in Facts.

Name of Nation_____

Capital_____

Boundaries (Bordering Nations and/or Bodies of Water):

1._____ 2._____ 3._____

    4._____ 5._____

Area: 240,535 sq. mi. **Comparative size:** slighty smaller than Texas
Terrain: plateau; scattered hills in the northeast and southwest
Climate: tropical
Geographic Note: landlocked; almost the exact center of Africa
Population: 3,642,739 people
Languages: (official) French and Sangho; tribal languages
Religion: indigenous beliefs 35%, Protestant 25%, Catholic 25%, Muslim 15%
Type of Government: republic
Exports: diamonds, timber, cotton, coffee, tobacco
Currency: Communaute Financiere Africaine franc (XAF)

FLAG DESCRIPTION: There are four equal horizonal bands: blue (top), white, green, and yellow. There is a vertical red band in center; there is a yellow, five-pointed star on the hoist side of the blue band.

Draw and Color Flag.

Hoist

Fly

Democratic Republic of Congo

Democratic
Republic of Congo

Mnemonic Device: When Al Cheery isn't reminiscing about his dad,
 Chad, courting Molly, trying to find a rhyming word for Niger, or
rubbing occo in his hair, or on his two knees, he is playing the bongo's.
<u>Democratic Republic of Congo</u> is depicted as the <u>lower half</u>, or legs of our
Clown Pictography. Listen to CD.

Use Map and Fill in Facts.

Name of Nation_____

Capital_____

Boundaries (Bordering Nations and/or Bodies of Water):

1._____ 2._____ 3._____

4._____ 5._____ 6._____

7._____ 8._____ 9._____

Area: 905,565 sq. mi. **Comparative size:** about one-fourth the size of the United States

Terrain: vast central basin; mountains in the east

Climate: tropical; hot and humid in equatorial river basin; cooler and drier in southern highlands

Geographic Note: Straddles Equator; has very narrow strip of land that controls the lower Congo River and is the only outlet to South Atlantic Ocean; dense tropical rain forest in central river basin and eastern highlands

Population: 55,225,478 people

Languages: (official) French; Lingala (trade language), Kingwana, Kikongo, Tshiluba

Religion: Catholic 50%, Protestant 20%, Kimbanguist 10%, Muslim 10%, indigenous beliefs and other 10%

Type of Government: dictatorship; presumably undergoing a transition to representative government

Exports: diamonds, copper, coffee, cobalt, crude oil

Currency: Congolese franc (CDF)

FLAG DESCRIPTION: It has a light blue field, with a large, yellow, five-pointed star in the center. It also has a columnar arrangement of six small, yellow, five-pointed stars along the hoist side.

Draw and Color Flag.

Hoist　　　　　　　　　　　　　　　　　　　　　Fly

Identify Flags of Clown Pictography.

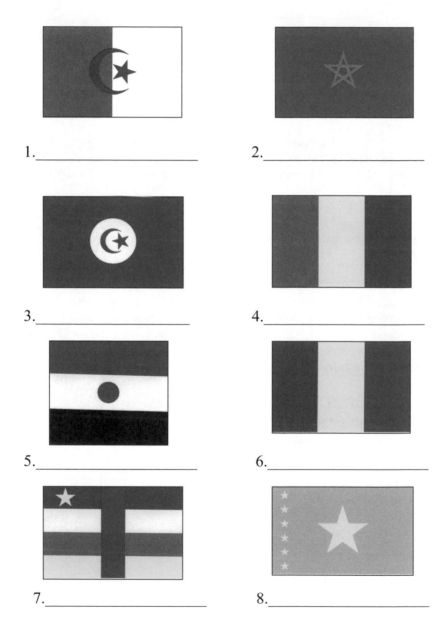

1._____

2._____

3._____

4._____

5._____

6._____

7._____

8._____

Identify Nations of Clown Pictography.

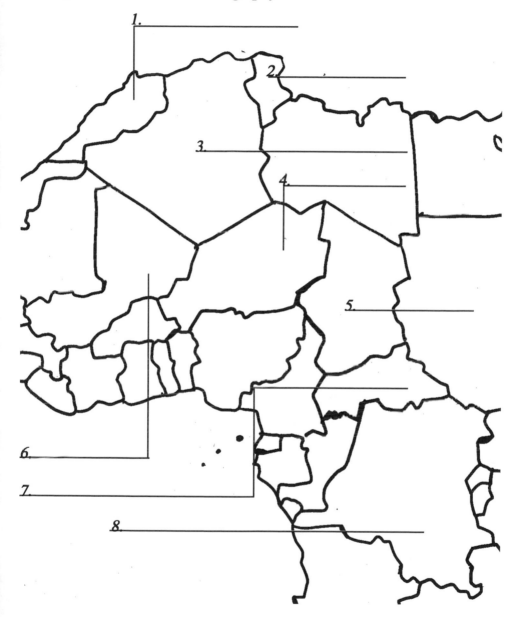

1.

2.

3.

4.

5.

6.

7.

8.

Africa
Hippo Wearing Shades

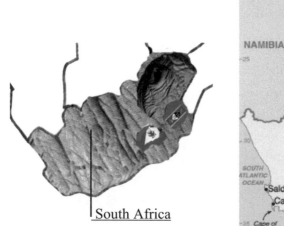

South Africa

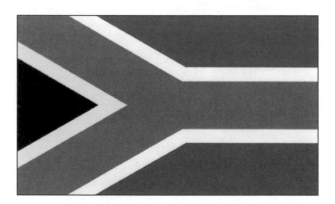

Mnemonic Device: <u>South Africa</u> is depicted as the main <u>body</u> of our cool Hippo Pictography. He looks so cool for the mere fact that he is wearing shades (sunglasses). If you turn the flag of South Africa so that the green band splits into a vertical Y; its two branching arms point us to the Hippo's two shaded eyes.

Use Map and Fill in Facts.

Name of Nation_____

Capital_____

Boundaries (Bordering Nations and/or Bodies of Water):

1._____ 2._____ 3._____

4._____ 5._____ 6._____

    7._____ 8._____

Area: 471,444 sq. mi. **Comparative size:** about twice the size of Texas

Terrain: interior plateau; hills around the rim, and narrow coastal plain

Climate: subtropical along east coast with sunny days, and cool nights; mostly semiarid

Geographic Note: completely surrounds Lesotho, and almost completely surrounds Swaziland

Population: 43,647,658 people

Languages: 11 official languages. Afrikaans, English, Ndebele, Pedi, Sotho, Swazi, Tsonga, Tswana, Venda, Xhosa, Zulu

Religion: Christian 68%; indigenous beliefs 28.5%; Muslim 2%, Hindu 1.5%

Type of Government: republic

Exports: gold, diamonds, platinum, other metals and minerals, machinery and equipment

Currency: rand (ZAR)

FLAG DESCRIPTION: There are two equal width horizontal bands of red (top) and blue. These bands are separated by a central green band which splits into a horizontal Y, the arms of which end at the corners of the hoist side; the Y embraces a black isosceles triangle from which the arms are separated by narrow yellow bands; the red and blue bands are separated from the green band and its arms by narrow white stripes.

Draw and Color Flag.

Hoist

Fly

Swaziland

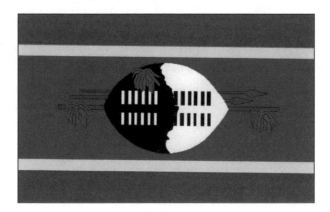

Mnemonic Device: When looking at our Hippo Pictography, <u>Swaziland</u>'s flag is depicted on one of the <u>sunglass lenses</u>. Since these two lenses are similar, keep in mind that Swaziland is the nation which borders Mozambique, and is <u>not</u> the one encircled by South Africa.

Use Map and Fill in Facts.

Name of Nation_____

Capital_____

Boundaries (Bordering Nations and/or Bodies of Water):

    1._____2._____

Area: 6,704 sq. mi. **Comparative size:** slighty smaller than New Jersey

Terrain: mostly mountains and hills; some moderately sloping plains

Climate: varies from tropical to near temperate

Geographic Note: landlocked; almost completely surrounded by South Africa

Population: 1,123,605 people

Languages: (official) English and siSwati

Religion: Zionist (a blend of Christianity and indigenous beliefs) 40%; Catholic 20%, Muslim 10%, Anglican, Bahai, Methodist, Mormon, Jewish and other 30%

Type of Government: monarchy; independent member of Commonwealth

Exports: soft drink concentrates, sugar, wood pulp, cotton yarn, refrigerators, citrus and canned fruit

Currency: lilangeni (SZL)

FLAG DESCRIPTION: There are three horizontal bands: blue (top), red (triple width), and blue. The red band is edged in yellow. Centered in the red band is a large black and white shield covering two spears, and a staff decorated with feather tassels-- all placed horizontally.

Draw and Color Flag.

Hoist

Fly

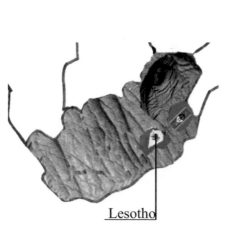

Lesotho

Mnemonic Device: Lesotho's flag is depicted on the left sunglass lens of our Hippo Pictography. If confused as to which lens is Swaziland and which is Lesotho, remember the Hippo's <u>Left lens is Lesotho</u>: the L of left is the L of Lesotho.

Use Map and Fill in Facts.

Name of Nation_____
Capital_____
Boundaries (Bordering Nations and/or Bodies of Water):
        1._____

Area: 11,761 sq. mi. **Comparative size:** slighty smaller than Maryland
Terrain: mostly highland with plateaus, hills, and mountains
Climate: temerate: cool to cold winters; hot, wet summers
Geographic Note: landlocked; completely surrounded by South Africa
Population: 2,207,954 people
Languages: (official) English; Sesotho (southern Sotho); Zulu, Xhosa
Religion: Christian 80%, indigenous beliefs 20%
Type of Government: parliamentary constitutional monarchy
Exports: manufactures 75% (clothing, footwear, road vehicles), wool and mohair, food and live animals
Currency: loti (LSL); South African rand (ZAR)

FLAG DESCRIPTION: Divided diagonally from the lower hoist side corner; the upper half is white, bearing the brown silhouette of a large shield with crossed spear and club. The lower half is a diagonal blue band with a green triangle in the corner.

Draw and Color Flag.

Hoist

Fly

Identify the Flags of Hippo Pictography.

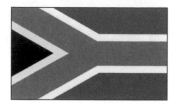 

1._____   2._____

3. _____

Identify Nations of Hippo Pictography.

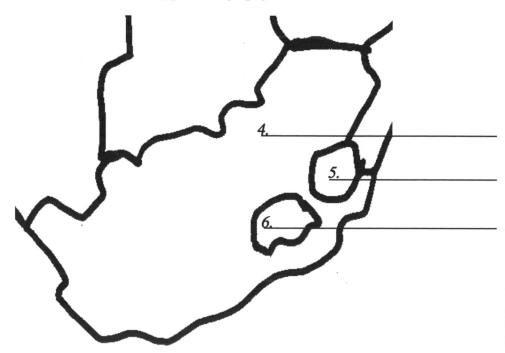

Africa
Snake

Senegal

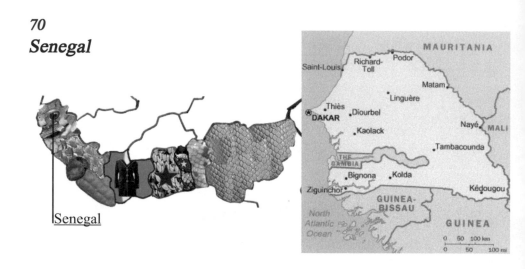

Senegal

Mnemonic Device: <u>Senegal</u> is depicted as the <u>head</u> of our Snake Pictography. The green star device on Senegal's flag can be thought of as that of the snake's eye. When you see the head of the snake, say, "SSSSSSSSSSSSSSenegal."

Use Map and Fill in Facts.

Name of Nation_____
Capital_____
Boundaries (Bordering Nations and/or Bodies of Water):
1._____ 2._____ 3._____
4._____ 5._____ 6._____

Area: 75,750 sq. mi. **Comparative size:** about the size of South Dakota
Terrain: low, rolling plains rising to foothills in southeast
Climate: tropical; hot and humid, rainy season from May to November.
Geographic Note: westernmost country on the African continent; The Gambia is almost an enclave of Senegal
Population: 10,589,571 people
Languages: (official) French; Wolof, Pulaar, Jola, Mandinka
Religion: Muslim 94%, Catholic 5%, indigenous beliefs 1%
Type of Government: republic under multiparty democratic rule
Exports: fish, groundnuts (peanuts), petroleum products, phosphates, cotton
Currency: Communaute Financiere Africaine franc (XOF)

FLAG DESCRIPTION: There are three equal vertical bands: green (hoist side), yellow, and red with a small, green, five-pointed star centered in the yellow band. It uses the popular pan-African colors of Ethiopia.

Draw and Color Flag.

Hoist

Fly

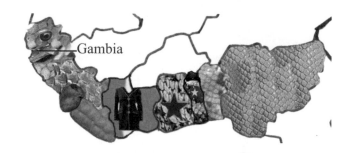

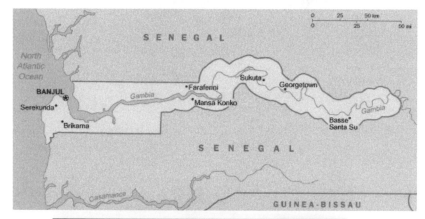

Mnemonic Device: Gambia is depicted as the <u>tongue</u> of our Snake Pictography. Gambia's flag has a horizontal orientation. The blue band between the white stripes is like an abstract representation of a thin, long tongue of a snake.

Use Map and Fill in Facts.

Name of Nation_____

Capital_____

Boundaries (Bordering Nations and/or Bodies of Water):

1._____ 2._____

Area: 4,361 sq. mi. **Comparative size:** twice the size of Delaware
Terrain: flood plain of the Gambia river
Climate: tropical; hot and humid, rainy season from June to November.
Geographic Note: almost an enclave of Senegal; smallest country in Africa
Population: 1,455,842 people
Languages: (official) English; Mandinka, Wolof, Fula, other indigenous languages
Religion: Muslim 90%; Christian 9%, indigenous beliefs 1%
Type of Government: republic under multiparty democratic rule
Exports: peanuts and peanut products, fish, cotton lint, palm kernels
Currency: dalasi (GMD)

FLAG DESCRIPTION: There are three equal horizontal bands: red (top), blue with white edges, and green.

Draw and Color Flag.

Hoist   Fly

Guinea-Bissau

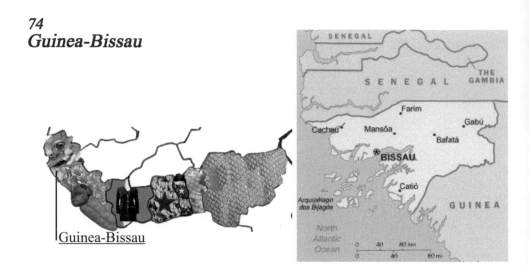

Guinea-Bissau

Mnemonic Device: <u>Guinea-Bissau</u> is depicted as the <u>throat</u> of our Snake Pictography. Imagine that this snake consumes a guinea pig for lunch. Upon swallowing it, the guinea pig bites him in the throat. The snake exclaims, "Guinea-Bis-owwwwww, that guinea pig bit me!!!

Use Map and Fill in Facts.

Name of Nation_____
Capital_____
Boundaries (Bordering Nations and/or Bodies of Water):
1._____2._____3._____

Area: 13,948 sq. mi. **Comparative size:** about three times the size of Connecticut
Terrain: low coastal plains; savanna in east
Climate: tropical; hot and humid, monsoon type rainy season from June to November.
Geographic Note: A small country that is swampy along its western coast.
Population: 1,345,479 people
Languages: (official) Portuguese; Crioulo, African languages
Religion: indigenous beliefs 50%, Muslim 45%, Christian 5%
Type of Government: republic under multiparty since mid-1991
Exports: cashew nuts 70%, shrimp, peanuts, palm kernels, sawn lumber
Currency: Communaute Financiere Africaine franc (XOF)

FLAG DESCRIPTION: There are two equal horizontal bands of yellow (top) and green with a vertical red band on the hoist side. There is a black, five-pointed star centered in the red band. It uses the popular pan-African colors of Ethiopia.

Draw and Color Flag.

Hoist

Fly

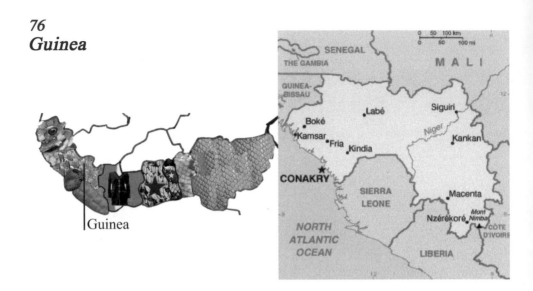

Mnemonic Device: After biting the snake's throat, the guinea pig becomes lodged <u>above and around the heart</u> of the snake. So in rememberance of this poor, little, guinea pig, we call this part of our Snake Pictography, <u>Guinea</u>.

Use Map and Fill in Facts.

Name of Nation_____
Capital_____
Boundaries (Bordering Nations and/or Bodies of Water):
1._____2._____3._____
      4._____5._____
      6._____7._____

Area: 95,000 sq. mi. **Comparative size:** about the size of Oregon
Terrain: generally flat coastal plains; hilly to mountainous interior
Climate: hot and humid: monsoon type rainy season from June to November
Geographic Note: The Niger and its tributary, the Milo, have their sources in the Guinean highlands
Population: 7,775,065 people
Languages: (official) French; each ethnic group has its own language
Religion: Muslim 85%, Christian 8%, indigenous beliefs 7%
Type of Government: republic
Exports: bauxite, alumina, gold, diamonds, coffee, fish, agricultural products
Currency: Guinean franc (GNF)

FLAG DESCRIPTION: There are three equal vertical bands: red (hoist side), yellow, and green. It uses the popular pan-African colors of Ethiopia.

Draw and Color Flag.

Hoist

Fly

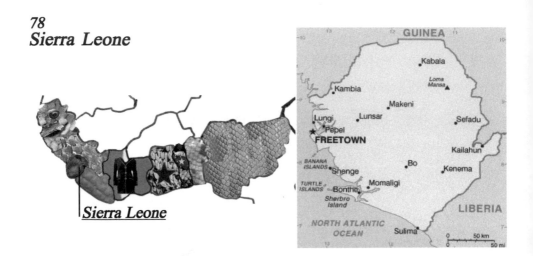

Sierra Leone

Mnemonic Device: Leon--in Latin means lion--Sierra Leone, the
lion-<u>hearted</u>. <u>Sierra Leone</u> is depicted as the <u>heart</u> of our Snake
Pictography. Listen to jingle on CD.

Use Map and Fill in Facts.

Name of Nation_____

Capital_____

Boundaries (Bordering Nations and/or Bodies of Water):

1._____ 2._____ 3._____

Area: 27,900 sq. mi. **Comparative size:** about the size of South Carolina
Terrain: mangrove swamps on coast; wooded-hill country, mountains in east
Climate: tropical; hot, humid; summer rainy season from May to December
Geographic Note: Rainfall along the coast can reach 195 inches/year. This makes it one of the wettest places along coastal, western Africa.
Population: 5,614,743 people
Languages: (official) English--used by literate minority; Mende in south; Temne in north; Krio spoken by 10% but understood by 95% of the people
Religion: Muslim 60%, indigenous beliefs 30%, Christian 10%
Type of Government: constitutional democracy
Exports: diamonds, rutile, cocoa, coffee, fish
Currency: leone (SLL)

FLAG DESCRIPTION: It has three equal horizontal bands: light green (top), white, and light blue.

Draw and Color Flag.

Hoist   Fly

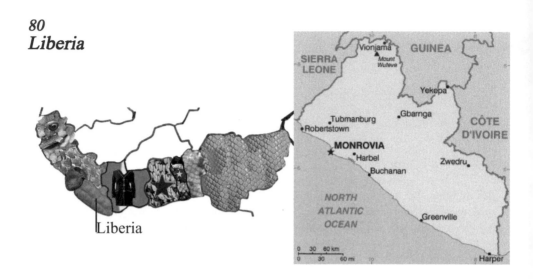

Mnemonic Device: Because it feels eerie to see a snake slither on its belly, <u>errie</u> <u>Liberia</u> is pronounced with quivering voice (as heard on CD) and is depicted as the <u>belly</u> of our Snake Pictography.

Use Map and Fill in Facts.

Name of Nation_____

Capital_____

Boundaries (Bordering Nations and/or Bodies of Water):

1._____ 2._____

3._____ 4._____

Area: 43,000 sq. mi. **Comparative size:** about the size of Tennessee
Terrain: flat to rolling coastal plains; low mountains in northeast
Climate: tropical; hot, humid; dry winters; heavy showers in summer
Geographic Note: Boardering the Atlantic Ocean, the coastline has many lagoons, swamps, and sandbars; inland is grassy plateau
Population: 3,288,198 people
Languages: (official) English 20%; some 20 ethnic group languages
Religion: Christian 40%; indigenous beliefs 40%; Muslim 20%
Type of Government: republic
Exports: rubber, timber, iron, diamonds, cocoa, coffee
Currency: Liberian dollar (LRD)

FLAG DESCRIPTION: It has eleven equal horizontal stripes of red (top and bottom) alternating with white. There is a white, five-pointed star on a blue square in the upper hoist-side corner. The design was based on the flag of the USA.

Draw and Color Flag.

Hoist   Fly

Cote d'Ivoire

Cote d'Ivoire

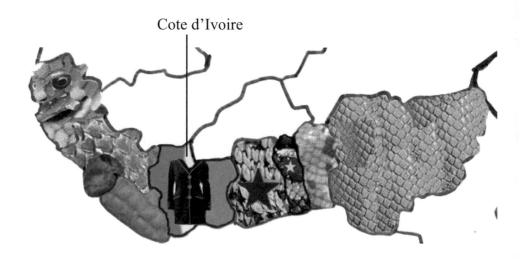

Mnemonic Device: When this snake sheds its skin, it covers the segment of his body that immediately preceeds his tail with a little coat (like wearing coattails). Also, this segment of the snake's body is colored similarly to the flag of <u>Cote d'Ivoire</u>. Hence, <u>this segment</u>, which has the orange to green backdrop, and a superimposed <u>coat</u>, is the nation of Cote d'Ivoire--also known as the Ivory Coast.

Use Map and Fill in Facts.

Name of Nation_____

Capital_____

Boundaries (Bordering Nations and/or Bodies of Water):

1._____ 2._____ 3._____

4._____ 5._____ 6._____

Area: 124,503 sq. mi. **Comparative size:** about the size of New Mexico

Terrain: mostly flat; some rolling plains; mountains in northwest

Climate: tropical along coast; semiarid in far north

Geographic Note: most inhabitants live along the sandy coastal region

Population: 16,804,784 people

Languages: (official) French; Dioula is most widely spoken; about 60 dialects.

Religion: Muslim 35-40%, indigenous 25-40%, Christian 20-30%

Type of Government: republic, multiparty presidential regime

Exports: cocoa 33%, coffee, timber, petroleum, cotton, bananas, pineapples, palm oil, fish

Currency: Cummunaute Financiere Africaine franc (XOF)

FLAG DESCRIPTION: There are three equal vertical bands: orange (hoist side), white, and green; similar to the flag of Ireland, and Italy. Its design was based on the flag of France.

Draw and Color Flag.

Hoist

Fly

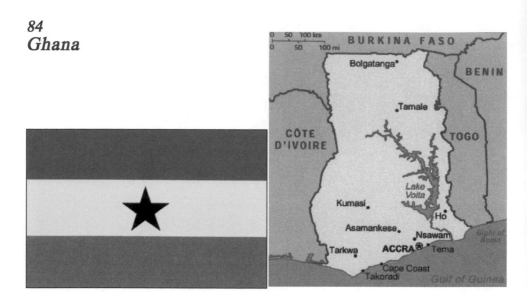

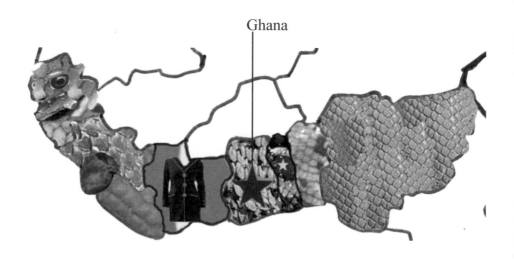

Ghana

Mnemonic Device: <u>Ghana</u> is depicted as the <u>first rattle</u> of our Snake Pictography. The black star device found on Ghana's flag is also found on this first rattle. Listen to CD for "Ghana-Togo-Benin-Nigeria" jingle.

Use Map and Fill in Facts.

Name of Nation_____

Capital_____

Boundaries (Bordering Nations and/or Bodies of Water):

      1._____ 2._____

   3._____ 4._____

Area: 92,099 sq. mi. **Comparative size:** about the size of Oregon

Terrain: mostly low plains with plateau in south-central area

Climate: tropical, relatively dry along southeast coast; hot and humid in southwest; hot and dry in north

Geographic Note: Lake Volta is the world's largest artificial lake.

Population: 20,244,154 people

Languages: (official) English; African languages e.g., Akan, Moshi-Dagomba, Twi

Religion: Christian 63%, indigenous beliefs 21%, Muslim 16%

Type of Government: constitutional democracy

Exports: gold, cocoa, timber, tuna, bauxite, aluminum, manganese ore, diamonds

Currency: cedi (GHC)

FLAG DESCRIPTION: There are three equal horizontal bands: red (top), yellow, and green with a large, black, five-pointed star centered in the yellow band. It uses the popular pan-African colors of Ethiopia. It is similar to the flag of Bolivia.

Draw and Color Flag.

Hoist

Fly

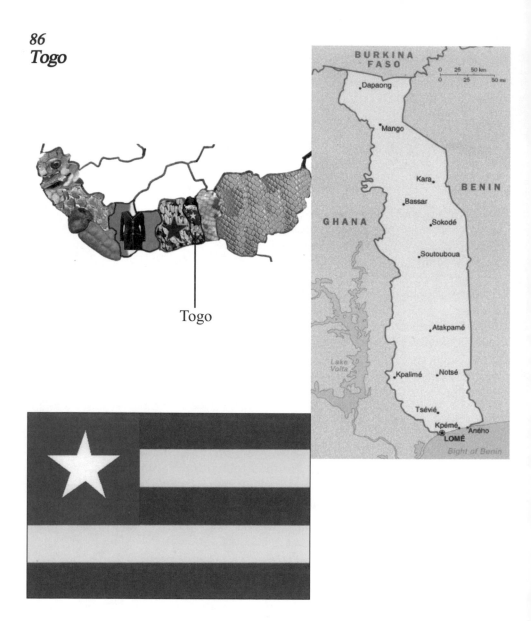

Togo

Mnemonic Device: <u>Togo</u> is depicted as the <u>second rattle</u> of our Snake Pictography. The white star device found on Togo's flag is also found on this second rattle. Listen to CD for the "Ghana-Togo-Benin-Nigeria" jingle.

Use Map and Fill in Facts.

Name of Nation_____

Capital_____

Boundaries (Bordering Nations and/or Bodies of Water):

      1._____ 2._____

      3._____ 4._____

Area: 21,925 sq. mi. **Comparative size:** about the size of West Virginia

Terrain: rolling savanna in north; southern plateau; low coast plain: lagoons, marshes

Climate: tropical; hot, humid in south; semiarid in north

Geographic Note: Climate varies from tropical to savanna because the country's length allows it to stretch through six distinct geographic regions.

Population: 5,285,501 people

Languages: (official) French; Ewe and Mina two major African languages in the south; Kabye and Dagomba are the two major African languages in the north

Religion: indigenous beliefs 51%, Christian 29%, Muslim 20%

Type of Government: republic; under transition to multiparty democratic rule

Exports: cotton, phosphates, coffee, cocoa

Currency: Communaute Financiere Africaine franc (XOF)

FLAG DESCRIPTION: There are five equal horizontal bands: green (top and bottom) alternating with yellow. There is a white, five-pointed star on a red square in the upper, hoist-side corner. It uses the popular pan-African colors of Ethiopia.

Draw and Color Flag.

Hoist

Fly

Benin

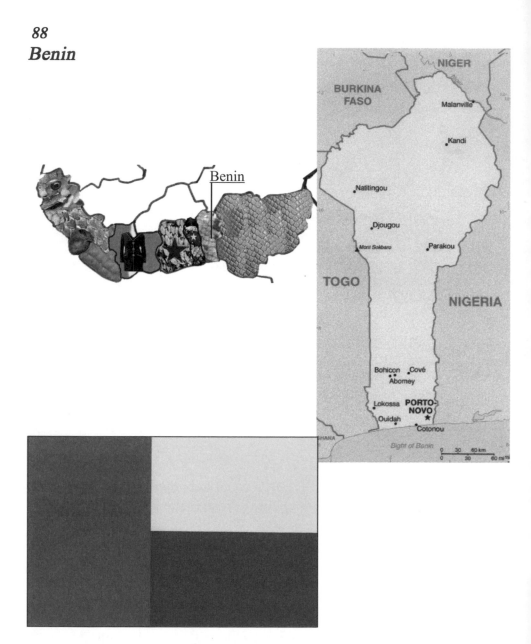

Mnemonic Device: <u>Benin</u> is depicted as the <u>third rattle</u> of our Snake Pictography. Listen to CD for the "Ghana-Togo-Benin-Nigeria" jingle.

Use Map and Fill in Facts.

Name of Nation_____
Capital_____
Boundaries (Bordering Nations and/or Bodies of Water):
1._____ 2._____ 3._____
        4._____ 5._____

Area: 43,484 sq. mi. **Comparative size:** about the size of Pennsylvania
Terrain: mostly flat to rolling hills; low mountains
Climate: tropical; hot, humid in south; semiarid in north
Geographic Note: Sandbanks create difficult access to a coast with no natural harbors, river mouths, or islands.
Population: 6,787,625 people
Languages: (official) French; Fon and Yoruba in the south; at least six tribal languages in the north
Religion: indigenous beliefs 50%, Christian 30%, Muslim 20%
Type of Government: republic; under multiparty democratic rule
Exports: cotton, crude oil, palm products, cocoa
Currency: Communaute Financiere Africaine franc (XOF)

FLAG DESCRIPTION: There are two equal horizontal bands: yellow (top) and red with a vertical green band on the hoist side.

Draw and Color Flag.

Hoist

Fly

Mnemonic Device: <u>Nigeria</u> is depicted as the <u>large</u>, and <u>final rattle</u> of our Snake Pictography. Listen to the CD for the "Ghana-Togo-Benin-Nigeria" jingle.

Use Map and Fill in Facts.

Name of Nation_____
Capital_____
Boundaries (Bordering Nations and/or Bodies of Water):
    1._____ 2._____ 3._____
          4._____ 5._____

Area: 356,668 sq. mi. **Comparative size:** about twice the size of California
Terrain: southern lowlands; central hills and plateaus; mountains in southeast, plains in the north
Climate: varies: equatorial in south; tropical in center; arid in north
Geographic Note: The Niger enters the country in the northwest and flows southward through tropical rain forests and swamps to its delta in the Gulf of Guinea.
Population: 129,934,911 people
Languages: (official) English; Hausa, Yoruba, Igbo (Ibo), Fulani
Religion: Muslim 50%, Christian 40%, indigenous beliefs 10%
Type of Government: republic; transitioning from military to civilian rule
Exports: petroleum and petroleum products 95%, cocoa, rubber
Currency: naira (NGN)

FLAG DESCRIPTION: There are three equal vertical bands: green (hoist side), white, and green.

Draw and Color Flag.

Hoist

Fly

Identify Flags of Snake Pictography.

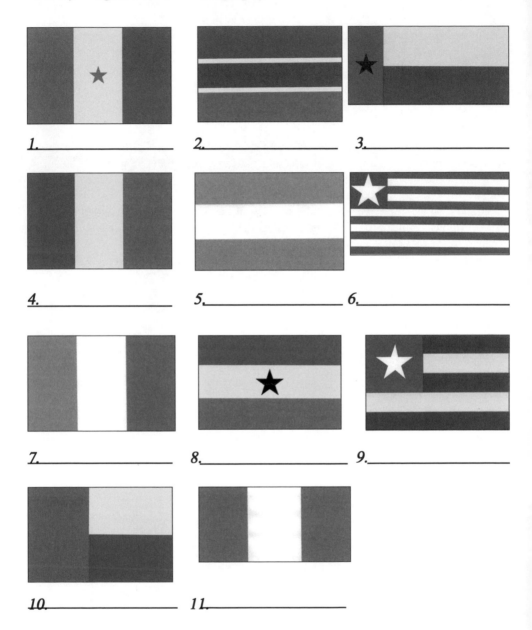

1._____

2._____

3._____

4._____

5._____

6._____

7._____

8._____

9._____

10._____

11._____

Identify Nations of Snake Pictography.

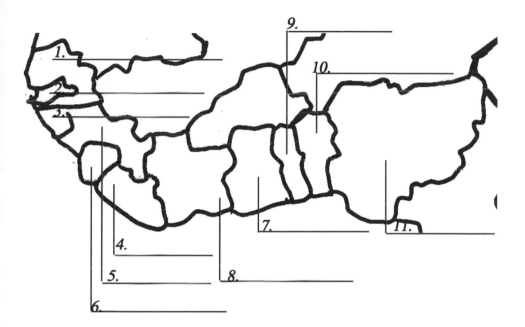

South America
Elephant Named Ana

Venezuela

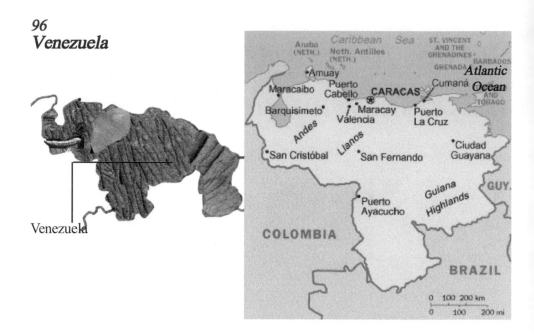

Venezuela

Mnemonic Device: <u>Venezuela</u> is depicted as the <u>whole elephant</u>, <u>except</u> for its <u>back leg</u>. When we look at the flag of Venezuela, we can see the curvature and coloring of its seven stars resembling that of an elephant's ivory tusk.

Use Map and Fill in the Facts.

Name of Nation_____
Capital_____
Boundaries (Bordering Nations and/or Bodies of Water):
1._____ 2._____ 3._____
4._____ 5._____

Area: 352,143 sq. mi. **Comparative size:** about twice the size of California
Terrain: Andes Mountains and Maracaibo Lowlands in northwest; central plains
(llanos); Guiana Highlands in southeast
Climate: tropical; hot and humid, more moderate in highlands
Geographic Note: Located on major sea and air routes linking North and South
America; Angel Falls in the Guiana Highlands is the world's highest waterfall
Population: 24,287,670 people
Languages: (official) Spanish; numerous indigenous dialects
Religion: nominally practicing Catholic 96%; Protestant 2%, other 2%
Type of Government: federal republic
Exports: petroleum, bauxite and aluminum, steel, chemicals, agricultural products,
basic manufactures
Currency: bolivar (VEB)

FLAG DESCRIPTION: There are three equal horizontal bands of yellow
(top), blue, and red with the coat of arms on the hoist side of the yellow
band, and an arc of seven, white, five-pointed stars centered in the blue
band.

Draw and Color Flag.

Hoist   Fly

Guyana

Mnemonic Device: <u>Guyana</u> is depicted as the <u>back leg</u> of our Elephant Pictography. This is a male elephant, but his name is Ana. Similar to a boy named Sue, this is a <u>guy</u> named <u>Ana</u>--<u>Guyana</u>.

Use Map and Fill in the Facts.

Name of Nation_____
Capital_____
Boundaries (Bordering Nations and/or Bodies of Water):
     1._____ 2._____
     3._____ 4._____

Area: 83,000sq. mi. **Comparative size:** slightly smaller than Idaho
Terrain: mostly rolling highlands; low coastal plain; savanna in south
Climate: tropical; hot and humid, moderated by trade winds; two rainy seasons (May to mid-August; mid-November to Mid-January)
Geographic Note: Third smallest country in South America after Suriname, Uruguay
Population: 698,209 people
Languages: (official) English; Amerindian dialects, Creole, Hindi, Urdu
Religion: Christian 50%, Hindu 35%, Muslim 10%, other 5%
Type of Government: republic with the Commonwealth
Exports: sugar, gold, bauxite/alumina, rice, shrimp, molasses, rum, timber
Currency: Guyanese dollar (GYD)

FLAG DESCRIPTION: A green field, with a red isosceles triangle (based on the hoist side). Superimposed on a long, yellow arrowhead. There is a narrow, black border between the red and yellow, and a narrow, white border between the yellow and the green.

Draw and Color Flag

Hoist   Fly

Identify the Flags of Elephant Pictography.

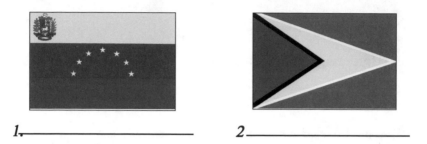

1.———————————— 2————————————

Identify the Nations of Elephant Pictography.

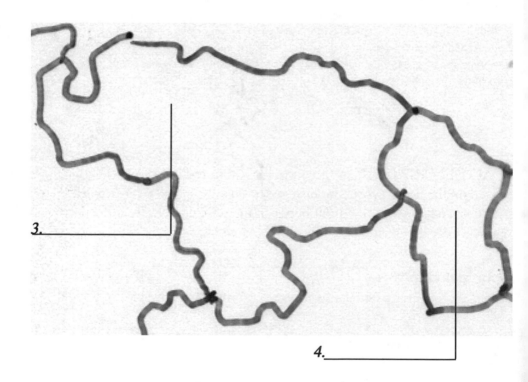

3.

4.

<u>South America</u>
Chili Pepper

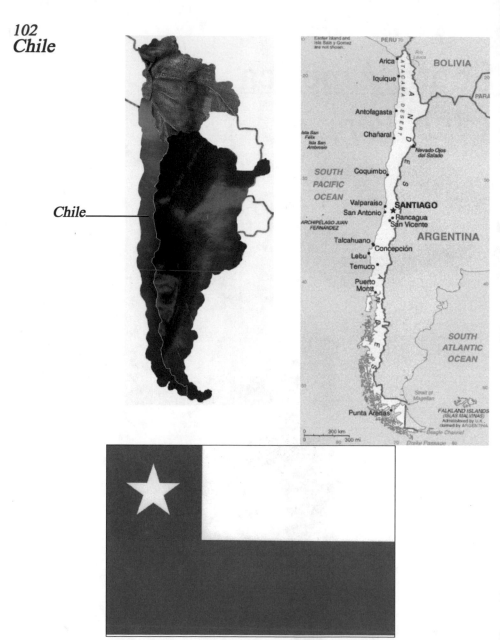

Chile

Mnemonic Device: <u>Chile</u> is depicted as the <u>orange stip</u> running along the edge of our Chili Pictography. Chile's western border is the Pacific Ocean, which is this pepper's water source. The flag of Chile resembles that of the state of Texas; where the weather isn't chili, but the eatin' is.

Use Map and Fill in Facts.

Name of Nation_____

Capital_____

Boundaries (Bordering Nations and/or Bodies of Water):

    1._____ 2._____

    3._____ 4._____

Area: 292,257 sq. mi. **Comparative size:** about twice the size of Montana

Terrain: low coastal mountains; fertile central valley; rugged Andes in east

Climate: temperate; desert in north; Mediterranean in central region

Geographic Note: Strategic location relative to sea lanes--between the Atlantic and Pacific Oceans e.g., Strait of Magellan, Beagle Channel; Atacama Desert is one of the world's driest regions

Population: 15,498,930 people

Languages: Spanish

Religion: Roman Catholic 89%, Protestant 11%

Type of Government: republic

Exports: copper, fish, fruits, paper and pulp, chemicals

Currency: Chilean peso (CLP)

FLAG DESCRIPTION: There are two equal horizontal bands: white (top) and red. There is a blue square the same height as the white band at the hoist-side end of the white band. The square bears a white, five-pointed star in the center. Its design was based on the flag of the USA.

Draw and Color Flag.

Hoist   Fly

Argentina

Mnemonic Device: <u>Argentina</u> is depicted as the <u>red, fleshy part</u> of our Chili Pepper Pictography. The device on Argentina's flag is a sun; which gives off the light necessary for this pepper to grow.

Use Map and Fill in Facts.

Name of Nation_____
Capital_____
Boundaries (Bordering Nations and/or Bodies of Water):
1._____ 2._____ 3._____
4._____ 5._____ 6._____

Area: 1,068,297 sq. mi. **Comparative size:** about three tenths the size of the USA
Terrain: rugged Andes along western border; rich plains of Pampas in northern half;
Climate: mostly temperate; arid in southeast
Geographic Note: Second largest country in South America (after Brazil); strategic
location relative to sea lanes between the South Atlantic and South Pacific Oceans
(Strait of Magellan, Beagle Channel, Drake Passage). Cerro Aconcagua is South
America's tallest mountain
Population: 37,812,817 people
Languages: (official) Spanish; English, Italian, German, French
Religion: Roman Catholic 92% (less than 20% practicing), Protestant 2%, Jewish 2%,
other 4%
Type of Government: republic
Exports: edible oils, fuels and energy, cereals, feed, motor vehicles
Currency: Argentine peso (ARS)

FLAG DESCRIPTION: There are three equal horizontal bands: light
blue (top), white, and light blue. Centered in the white band is a radiant,
yellow sun with a human face known as the Sun of May.

Draw and Color Flag.

Hoist   Fly

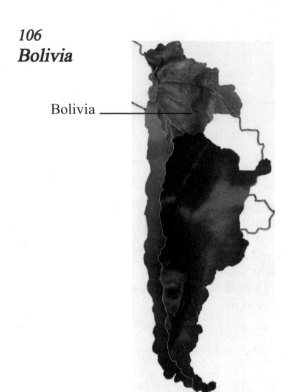

Bolivia ——————

Mnemonic Device: <u>Bolivia</u> is depicted as the <u>leaves</u> of our Chili Pepper Pictography. The Chili Pepper's leaves are plucked off the pepper and left in a bowl. Bowl of leaves...bowl-leaf-ia.

Use Map and Fill in Facts.

Name of Nation_____
Capital_____
Boundaries (Bordering Nations and/or Bodies of Water):
1._____ 2._____ 3._____
    4._____ 5._____

Area: 424,163 sq. mi. **Comparative size:** about three times the size of Montana
Terrain: rugged Andes Mountains with highland plateau; lowland plains of the
Amazon Basin
Climate: varies with altitude; humid and tropical to cold and semiarid
Geographic Note: landlocked; shares control with Peru of Lago Titicaca--world's
highest navigable lake (elevation 3,805 m)
Population: 8,445,134 people
Languages: (official) Spanish, Quechua, and Aymara
Religion: Roman Catholic 95%, Protestant (Evangelical Methodist) 5%
Type of Government: republic
Exports: soybeans, natural gas, zinc, gold, wood
Currency: Boliviano (BOB)

FLAG DESCRIPTION: There are three equal horizontal bands: red
(top), yellow, and green with the coat of arms centered on the yellow band.

Draw and Color Flag.

Hoist

Fly

Identify Flags of Chili Pepper Pictography.

1._____

2._____

3._____

South America
"Guay" Game

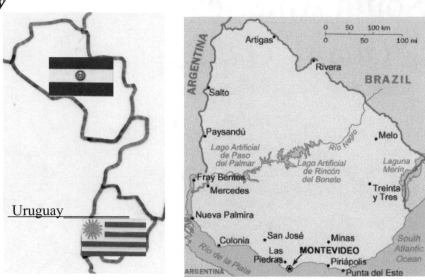

Uruguay

Mnemonic Device: The <u>area outlined</u> behind Uruguay's flag is the nation of <u>Uruguay.</u> The Sun of May's human face used on its flag says, "You're a guay." This is the material you will use for bantering a partner.

Use Map and Fill in Facts.

Name of Nation_____

Capital_____

Boundaries (Bordering Nations and/or Bodies of Water):

1._____ 2._____ 3._____

Area: 68,037 sq. mi. **Comparative size:** about the size of the state of Washington

Terrain: mostly rolling plains; fertile coastal lowland

Climate: warm temperate

Geographic Note: second-smallest South American country (after Suriname); three-quarters of the country is grassland, ideal for cattle and sheep raising

Population: 3,386,575 people

Languages: Spanish, Portunol, or Brazilero (Portuguese-Spanish mix on the Brazilian frontier)

Religion: Roman Catholic 66%, (less than half of adults attend church regularly), Protestant 2%, Jewish 1%, nonprofessing or other 31%

Type of Government: constitutional republic

Exports: meat, rice, leather products, wool, vehicles, dairy products

Currency: Uruguayan peso (UYU)

FLAG DESCRIPTION: There are nine equal horizontal stripes of white (top and bottom) alternating with blue. There is a white square in the upper, hoist-side corner. Within the square is a yellow sun bearing a human face known as the Sun of May with 16 rays that alternate triangular and wavy.

Draw and Color Flag.

Hoist   Fly

Paraguay

Paraguay

Mnemonic Device: Find a partner and tell him what the May Sun on Uruguay's flag says, "You're a guay." Let the partner respond, "no, I'm not a guay, you're a guay." Say again, "no, you're a guay." Let your partner respond, "no, you're a guay." Continue in this way awhile, then one of you exclaims, "O.K., O.K., we're a <u>pair</u> <u>a</u> <u>guay,</u> <u>Paraguay.</u>" When looking at both Uruguay, and Paraguay, note that a "pair a' guay" take up more space than does one guay. Hence, the <u>larger nation</u> is <u>Paraguay</u>.

Use Map and Fill in Facts.

Name of Nation_____

Capital_____

Boundaries (Bordering Nations and/or Bodies of Water):

1._____ 2._____ 3._____

Area: 157,047 sq. mi. **Comparative size:** about the size of California

Terrain: marshy plain near the river, and dry forest and thorny scrub elsewhere; grassy plains and wooded hills east of Rio Paraguay

Climate: subtropical to temperate; substaintial rainfall in the east; semiarid in the west

Geographic Note: landlocked; lies between Argentina, Bolivia, and Brazil; population concentrated in southern part of country

Population: 5,884,491 people

Languages: (official) Spanish and Guarani

Religion: Roman Catholic 90%, Mennonite, and other Protestant

Type of Government: constitutional republic

Exports: electricity, soybeans, feed, cotton, meat, edible oils

Currency: guarani (PYG)

FLAG DESCRIPTION: There are three equal, horizontal bands: red (top), white, and blue with an emblem centered in the white band. Unlike most flags in that the emblem is different on each side. The obverse (hoist side is on the left) bears the national coat of arms (a yellow, five-pointed star within a green wreath, encircled by the words REPUBLICA DEL PARAGUAY, all within two circles. On the reverse side, the emblem bears the seal of the treasury, and not the national coat of arms.

Draw and Color Flag.

Hoist   Fly

Identify the Flags of "Guay" Game Pictography.

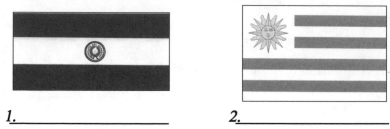

1._____   2._____

Identify Nations of Chili Pepper and "Guay" Game Pictographies.

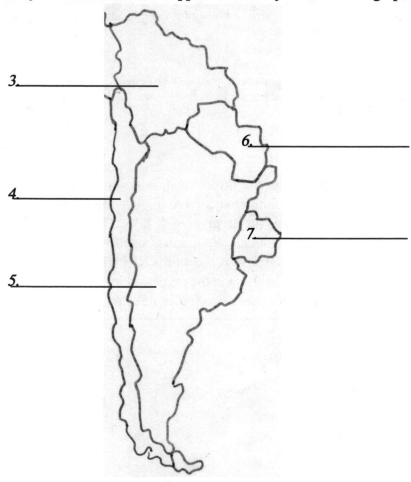

3._____

6._____

4._____

7._____

5._____

South America

Jester

Peru

Mnemonic Device: Our Jester Pictography likes to play a game with his cat. His cat in not visible because he is hidden under the Jester's arm. Yet we know the Jester's cat is there because there's a whole lot of purring going on. Therefore, the Jester's arm (from whence the purring comes) is called Purrrrr-u, Peru.

Use Map and Fill in Facts.

Name of Nation_____
Capital_____
Boundaries (Bordering Nations and/or Bodies of Water):
1._____2._____3._____
4._____5._____6._____

Area: 496,224 sq. mi. **Comparative size:** about the size of Alaska
Terrain: western coastal plain (costa), high and rugged Andes in center (sierra), eastern
lowland jungle of Amazon Basin (selva)
Climate: tropical in east; dry desert in west; temperate to very cold in Andes
Geographic Note: shares control with Bolivia of Lago Titicaca; remote Lake McIntyre
is the ultimate source of the Amazon River
Population: 27,949,639 people
Languages: (official) Spanish and Quechua; Aymara
Religion: Roman Catholic 90%, other 10%
Type of Government: constitutional republic
Exports: fish and fish products, gold, copper, zinc, crude petroleum and byproducts,
lead, coffee, sugar, cotton
Currency: nuevo sol (PEN)

FLAG DESCRIPTION: There are three equal, vertical bands: red (hoist
side), white, and red with the coat of arms centered in the white band. The
coat of arms features a shield bearing a vicuna, cinchona tree (source of
quinine), and a yellow cornucopia spilling out gold coins, all framed by a
green wreath.

Draw and Color Flag.

Hoist   Fly

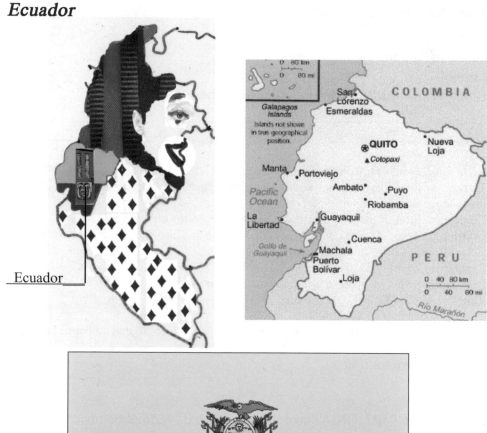

Ecuador

Mnemonic Device: Continuing with the cat game... this Jester loves to carry his purring cat under his arm (Peru), until he reaches a door. As soon as he comes to a door, the cat gets put on the floor, so that the Jester can lift his arms straight over his head with his elbows as close to his ears as possible. The jester's shoulder is adorned with an epaulet that is embroidered with a <u>door</u> for Ecua-door. It is his shoulder that does the work to lift his arms when he reaches a door; the jester's <u>shoulder</u> is <u>Ecuador</u>.

Use Map and Fill in Facts.

Name of Nation_____
Capital_____
Boundaries (Bordering Nations and/or Bodies of Water):
1._____2._____3._____

Area: 109,483 sq. mi. **Comparative size:** about the size of Nevada
Terrain: coastal plain (costa), inter-Andean centeral highlands (sierra), and flat to rolling eastern jungle (oriente)
Climate: tropical along coast, cool inland at higher elevations; tropical in Amazonian jungle lowlands
Geographic Note: the highest active volcano in world is Cotopaxi in the Andes
Population: 13,447,494 people
Languages: (official) Spanish; Amerindian languages (especially Quechua)
Religion: Roman Catholic 95%, other 5%
Type of Government: republic
Exports: petroleum, bananas, shrimp, coffee, cocoa, cut flowers, fish
Currency: US dollar (USD)

FLAG DESCRIPTION: There are three horizontal bands: yellow (top, double width), blue, and red with the coat of arms superimposed at the center of the flag. It is similar to the flag of Colombia.

Draw and Color Flag.

Hoist   Fly

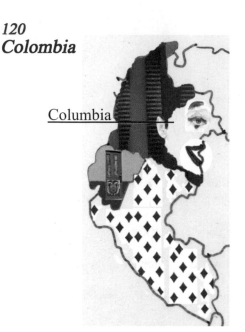

Columbia

Mnenomic Device: With his arms extended above his head, and as close to his ears as possible, the jester begins to chant.... "Be a column, be a column, be a column." Try this yourself and you shall encounter an auditory illusion. Said enough times, the stress in the words reverse themselves so that <u>be</u> a column, becomes <u>Co</u>lumbia. <u>Columbia</u> is depicted as the jester's <u>face</u> and <u>hat</u>.

Use Map and Fill in Facts.

Name of Nation_____
Capital_____
Boundaries (Bordering Nations and/or Bodies of Water):
1._____2._____3._____
    4._____5._____
    6._____7._____

Area: 439,734 sq. mi. **Comparative size:** about three times the size of Montana
Terrain: flat coastal lowlands, central highlands, high Andes Mountains, eastern plains
Climate: tropical along coast and eastern plains, cooler in highlands
Geographic Note: only South American country with coastlines on both North Pacific Ocean and Caribbean Sea
Population: 41,008,227 people
Languages: Spanish
Religion: Roman Catholic 90%, other 10%
Type of Government: republic; executive branch dominates government structure
Exports: petroleum, coffee, coal, apparel, bananas, cut flowers
Currency: Colombian peso (COP)

FLAG DESCRIPTION: There are three horizontal bands: yellow (top, double width), blue, and red. It is similar to Ecuador's flag, except shorter, and without the coat of arms device.

Draw and Color Flag

Hoist   Fly

Identify Flags of Jester Pictography.

1._____

2._____

3._____

Identify Nations of Jester Pictography.

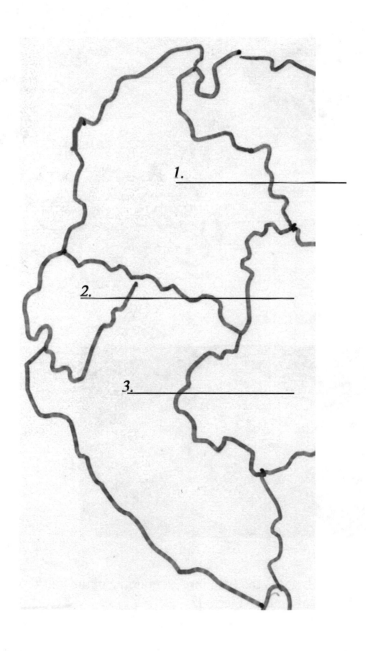

1. _____

2. _____

3. _____

South America *Brazil*

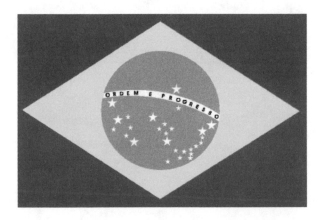

Mnemonic Device: Brazil is the fifth largest country in the world, and comprises nearly half of South America.

Use Map and Fill in Facts.

Name of Nation_____

Capital_____

Boundaries (Bordering Nations and/or Bodies of Water):

1._____ 2._____ 3._____

4._____ 5._____ 6._____

7._____ 8._____ 9._____

   10._____ 11._____

Area: 3,286,475 sq. mi. **Comparative size:** slightly smaller than the USA

Terrain: mostly flat to rolling lowlands in north; some plains, hills, mountains, and narrow coastal belt

Climate: mostly tropical, but temperate in south

Geographic Note: largest country in South America, shares common boundaries with every South American countries except for Chile and Ecuador

Population: 176,029,560 people

Languages: (official) Portuguese; Spanish, English, French

Religion: (nominal) Roman Catholic 80%, other 20%

Type of Government: federative republic

Exports: manufactures, iron ore, soybeans, footwear, coffee, autos

Currency: real (BRL)

FLAG DESCRIPTION: It has a green field with a large yellow diamond in the center bearing a blue celestial globe with 27 white, five-pointed stars--one for each state and the Federal District. These stars are arranged in the same pattern as the night sky over Brazil; the globe has a white, equatorial band with the motto ORDEM E PROGRESSO (Order and Progress).

Draw and Color Flag.

Hoist   Fly

North America
United States of America

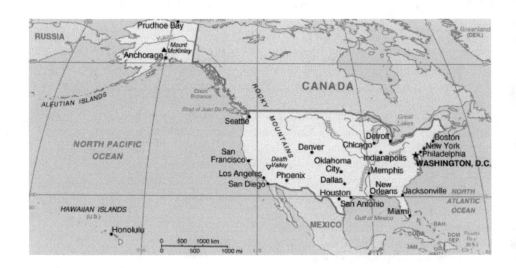

Use Map and Fill in Facts.

Name of Nation_____
Capital_____
Boundaries of contiguous 48 states
(Bordering Nations and/or Bodies of Water):
1._____2._____3._____
    4._____5._____

Area: 3,618,768 sq. mi. **Comparative size:** about half the size of Russia; about three-tenths the size of Africa; about half the size of South America (slightly larger than Brazil); slightly larger than China; about two and a half times size of Western Europe
Terrain: vast central plain, mountains in west, hills and low mountains in east; rugged mountains and broad river valleys in Alaska; rugged, volcanic topography in Hawaii
Climate: mostly temperate, but tropical in Hawaii and Florida; arctic in Alaska
Geographic Note: world's third-largest country by size (after Russia and Canada) and by population (after China and India)
Population: 280,562,489 people
Languages: English; Spanish spoken by a sizable minority
Religion: Protestant 56%, Roman Catholic 28%, Jewish 2%, other 4% none 10%
Type of Government: federal republic; strong democratic tradition
Exports: capital goods, automobiles, industrial supplies and raw materials, consumer goods, agricultural products
Currency: US dollar (USD)
FLAG DESCRIPTION: There are thirteen equal horizontal stripes of red (top and bottom) alternating with white. There is a blue rectangle in the upper hoist-side corner bearing 50 small, white, five-pointed stars arranged in nine offset rows of five stars. The 50 stars represent the 50 states; the 13 stripes represent the 13 original colonies--known as Old Glory.

Draw and Color Flag.

Hoist

Fly

North America *Canada*

Use Map and Fill in Facts.

Name of Nation_____

Capital_____

Boundaries (Bordering Nations and/or Bodies of Water):

    1._____ 2._____

    3._____ 4._____

Area: 3,851,792 sq. mi. **Comparative size:** slightly larger than the USA
Terrain: mostly plains with mountains in west and lowlands in southeast
Climate: varies from temperate in south to subarctic, and arctic in north
Geographic Note: second-largest country in the world (after Russia); strategic location between Russia and US via north polar route; about 85% of population is concentrated within 300 km of the US and Canadian border.
Population: 31,902,268 people
Languages: (official) English 59.3% and French 23.2%; other 17.5%
Religion: Roman Catholic 46%, Protestant 36%, other 18%
Type of Government: confederation with parliamentary democracy
Exports: motor vehicles and parts, industrial machinery, aircraft, telecommunications equipment; chemicals, plastics, fertilizers, wood pulp, timber, crude petroleum, natural gas, electricity, aluminum
Currency: Canadian dollar (CAD)

FLAG DESCRIPTION: There are three vertical bands of red (hoist-side), white (double width, square), and red with a red maple leaf centered in the white band.

Draw and Color Flag.

Hoist   Fly

North America _Mexico_

Use Map and Fill in Facts.

Name of Nation_____
Capital_____
Boundaries (Bordering Nations and/or Bodies of Water):
1._____ 2._____ 3._____
4._____ 5._____ 6._____

Area: 761,602 sq. mi. **Comparative size:** about three times the size of Texas
Terrain: high, rugged mountains; low coastal plains, high plateaus, desert
Climate: varies from tropical to desert
Geographic Note: strategic location on southern border of USA; corn (maize), one of
the world's major grain crops, is thought to have originated in Mexico
Population: 103,400,165 people
Languages: Spanish, various Mayan, Nanuati, and other regional indigenous languages
Religion: nominally Roman Catholic 89%, Protestant 6%, other 5%
Type of Government: federal republic
Exports: manufactured goods, oil and oil products, silver, fruits, vegetables, coffee,
cotton
Currency: Mexican peso (MXN)

FLAG DESCRIPTION: There are three equal vertical bands: green
(hoist side), white, and red. The coat of arms (an eagle perched on a cactus
with a snake in its beak) is centered in the white band.

Draw and Color Flag.

Hoist   Fly

Identify Flags of North America.

1. _____   2. _____   3. _____

Identify Nations of North America.

4. _____

5. _____

6. _____

Central America

Man Eating
* Giant Ice Cream Cone*

Guatemala

Guatemala

Mnemonic Device: During this man's visit to Guatemala, he bought himself a beautiful, pearled jacket. He thought he looked "bad" in his new threads.--The word for bad in spanish is "mala".--So when he checked himself out in the mirror, and saw such a cool jacket, he exclaimed, "What a mala dude, man!" Guatamala is depicted as the jacket in our Man and Ice Cream Pictography.

Use Map and Fill in Facts.

Name of Nation_____

Capital_____

Boundaries (Bordering Nations and/or Bodies of Water):

1._____ 2._____ 3._____

4._____ 5._____ *(Caribbean Sea)

Area: 42,042 sq. mi. **Comparative size:** about the size of Tennessee
Terrain: mostly mountains with narrow coastal plains and rolling limestone plateau
Climate: tropical; hot, humid in lowlands; cooler in highlands
Geographic Note: no natural harbor on west coast
Population: 13,314,079 people
Languages: Spanish 60%, Amerindian languages 40% e.g.Quiche, Cakchiquel, Kekchi
Religion: Roman Catholic 62%, Protestant 30%, indigenous Mayan belief and other 8%
Type of Government: constitutional democratic republic
Exports: coffee, sugar, bananas, fruits and vegetables, cardamom, meat, apparel, petroleum, electricity
Currency: quetzal (GTQ), US dollar (USD), others allowed

FLAG DESCRIPTION: There are three equal vertical bands: light blue (hoist side), white, and light blue with the coat of arms centered in the white band. The coat of arms includes a green and red quetzal (the national bird) and a scroll bearing the inscription: LIBERTAD 15 DE SEPTIEMBRE DE 1821 (original date of independence from Spain). This is all superimposed on a pair of crossed rifles and a pair of crossed swords which are framed by a wreath.

Draw and Color Flag.

Hoist   Fly

El Salvador

El Salvador

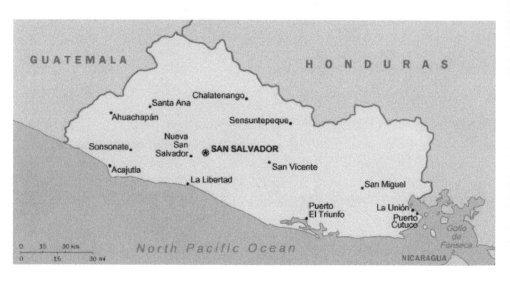

Mnemonic Device: Our "mala" dude sporting his new jacket travels to El Salvador. Here, through a window, he spies pearl-covered boots. However, what he really is seeing is an exhibit of <u>Salvador</u> Dali's paintings; his matching boots are really only paint on canvas. So the man buys Dali's painting of the boots, and has a cobbler replicate them!! <u>El Salvador</u> is depicted as the <u>boot</u> in our Man and Ice Cream Pictography.

Use Map and Fill in Facts.

Name of Nation_____

Capital_____

Boundaries (Bordering Nations and/or Bodies of Water):

1._____2._____3._____

Area: 8,124 sq. mi. **Comparative size:** about the size of Massachusetts
Terrain: mostly mountains with narrow coastal belt and central plateau
Climate: tropical on coast; temperate in uplands, rainy season May to October
Geographic Note: smallest Central American country and only one without a coastline on Caribbean Sea
Population: 6,353,681 people
Languages: Spanish, Nahua (among some Amerindians)
Religion: Roman Catholic 83%
Type of Government: republic
Exports: offshore assembly exports, coffee, sugar, shrimp, textiles, chemicals, electricity
Currency: Salvadoran colon (SVC); US dollar (USD)

FLAG DESCRIPTION: There are three equal horizontal bands: blue (top), white, and blue with the national coat of arms centered in the white band. The coat of arms features a round emblem encircled by the words REPUBLICA DE EL SALVADOR EN LA AMERICA CENTRAL.

Draw and Color Flag.

Hoist

Fly

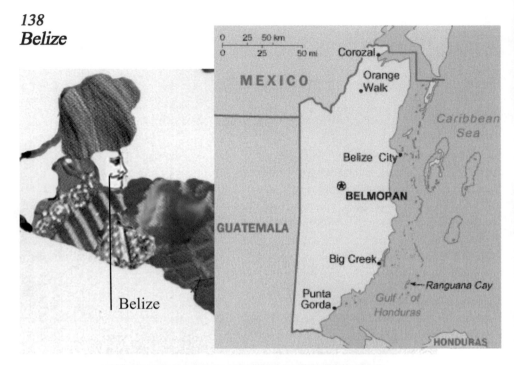

Belize

Mnemonic Device: Sporting a heavily beaded jacket and boots, makes the man a bit too warm. To cool off he asks each of the ice cream shops in Belize to make him an ice cream cone. Unfortunately, Belize is completely out of ice cream. He pleads with them, "please, please, Belize." Those in <u>Belize</u> who see his <u>face</u>, take pity on him as he continues to plea, "please, please, Belize." <u>Belize</u> is depicted as the <u>face</u> of our Man and Ice Cream Pictography.

Use Map and Fill in Facts.

Name of Nation_____
Capital_____
Boundaries (Bordering Nations and/or Bodies of Water):
1._____2._____3._____

Area: 8,867 sq. mi. **Comparative size:** about the size of Massachusetts
Terrain: flat, swampy coastal plain; low mountains in south
Climate: tropical; very hot and humid; rainy season from May to November
Geographic Note: only country in Central America without a coastline on the North Pacific Ocean
Population: 262,999 people
Languages: (official) English; Spanish, Mayan, Garifuna (Carib), Creole
Religion: Roman Catholic 49.6%, Protestant 27%, none 9.4%, other 14%
Type of Government: parliamentary democracy
Exports: sugar, bananas, citrus, clothing, fish products, molasses, wood
Currency: Belizean dollar (BZD)

FLAG DESCRIPTION: It has a blue field with a narrow red stripe along the top and the bottom edges. Centered is a large, white disk bearing the coat of arms. The coat of arms features a shield flanked by two workers in front of a mahogany tree with the related motto SUB UMBRA FLOREO (I Flourish in the Shade) on a scroll at the bottom, all encircled by a green garland.

Draw and Color Flag.

Hoist

Fly

Honduras

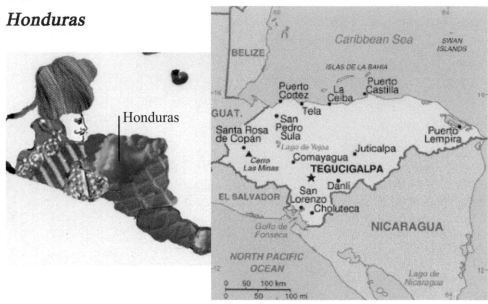

Honduras

Mnemonic Device: The ice cream shops in Belize, explain that the very best banana-strawberry ice cream is found across the border in Honduras-- the original "banana republic". Since banana-strawberry ice cream is the man's absolute favorite flavor, he travels to Honduras for the most humongous ice cream cone ever!!! <u>Honduras</u> is depicted as the<u> ice cream scoop</u> of our Man and Ice Cream Pictography.

Use Map and Fill in Facts.

Name of Nation_____
Capital_____
Boundaries (Bordering Nations and/or Bodies of Water):
1._____2._____3._____
　　　4._____5._____

Area: 43,278 sq. mi. **Comparative size:** slightly larger than Tennessee
Terrain: narrow coastal plains; mostly mountains in interior
Climate: subtropical in lowlands, temperate in mountains
Geographic Note: has only a short Pacific coast but a long Caribbean shoreline,
including the virtually uninhabited eastern Mosquito Coast
Population: 6,560,608 people
Languages: Spanish, Amerindian dialects
Religion: Roman Catholic 97%, Protestant minority
Type of Government: democratic constitutional republic
Exports: coffee, bananas, shrimp, lobster, meat; zinc, lumber
Currency: lempira (HNL)

FLAG DESCRIPTION: There are three equal horizontal bands: blue (top), white, and blue. It has five blue, five-pointed stars arranged in an X pattern centered in the white band. The stars represent the members of the former Federal Republic of Central America--Costa Rica, El Salvador, Guatemala, Honduras, and Nicaragua.

Draw and Color Flag.

Hoist

Fly

Nicaragua

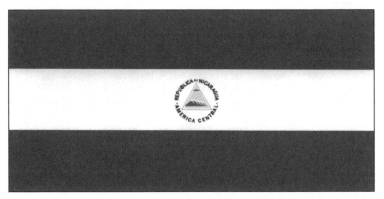

Mnemonic Device: Upon seeing this confectionary delight, the man, without hesitation, slides himself right into the top of it!!! Well, this cracks the cone so that it consists of a top half and a bottom half. Nicaragua is depicted as the top half of the ice cream cone in our Man and Ice Cream Pictography. Nicaragua's flag has a triangular device which is the same shape as an inverted sugar cone.

Use Map and Fill in Facts.

Name of Nation_____
Capital_____
Boundaries (Bordering Nations and/or Bodies of Water):
1._____ 2._____
    3._____ 4._____

Area: 50,193 sq. mi. **Comparative size:** slightly smaller than the state of New York
Terrain: extensive Atlantic coastal plains rising to central interior mountains; narrow
Pacific coastal plain interrupted by volcanoes
Climate: tropical in lowlands, cooler in highlands
Geographic Note:largest country in Central America; contains the largest freshwater
body in Central America, Lago de Nicaragua
Population: 5,023,818 people
Languages: (official) Spanish, English and indigenous language on Atlantic coast
Religion: Roman Catholic 85%, Protestant minority
Type of Government: republic
Exports: coffee, shrimp and lobster, cotton, tobacco, beef, sugar, bananas; gold
Currency: gold cordoba (NIO)

FLAG DESCRIPTION: There are three equal horizontal bands: blue
(top), white, and blue. It has the national coat of arms centered in the
white band. The coat of arms features a triangle encircled by the words
REPUBLICA DE NICARAGUA on the top and AMERICA CENTRAL on
the bottom.

Draw and Color Flag.

Hoist   Fly

Costa Rica

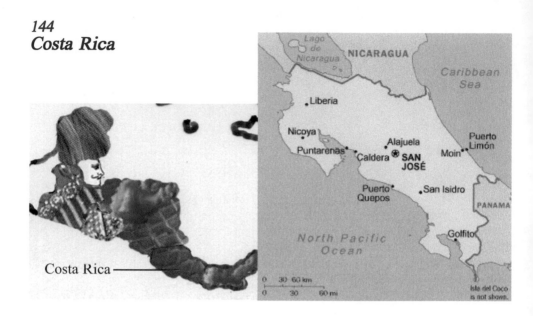

Costa Rica ———

Mnemonic Device: Costa Rica is depicted as the <u>bottom half</u> of the sugar <u>cone</u> in our Man and Ice Cream Pictography. The center of Costa Rica is littered with volcanic <u>cones</u>.

Use Map and Fill in Facts.

Name of Nation_____
Capital_____
Boundaries (Bordering Nations and/or Bodies of Water):
1._____2._____
    3._____   4._____

Area: 19,575 sq. mi. **Comparative size:** slightly smaller than West Virginia
Terrain: coastal plains separated by rugged mountains including over 100 volcanic cones, of which several are major volcanoes
Climate: tropical and subtropical; rainy season is May to Novermber
Geographic Note: four volcanoes, two of them active, rise near the capital of San Jose in the center of the country; one of the volcanoes, Irazu, erupted destructively in 1963-65
Population: 3,834,934 people
Languages: (official) Spanish; English spoken around Puerto Limon
Religion: Roman Catholic 76.3%, Evangelical 13.7%, other Protestant .7%, Jehovah's Witnesses 1.3%, other 4.8%, none 3.2%
Type of Government: democratic republic
Exports: coffee, bananas, sugar; pineapples; textiles, electronic components, medical equipment
Currency: Costa Rican colon (CRC)

FLAG DESCRIPTION: There are five horizontal bands: blue (top), white, red (double width), white, and blue. The coat of arms is in a white disk on the hoist side of the red band.

Draw and Color Flag.

Hoist

Fly

Panama

Mnemonic Device: When the ice cream cone cracks, the banana-straw-berry ice cream begins to run out the bottom of the cone. Luckily the man's mother is in a nearby kitchen. So the man calls to her saying: "Ma, get me a <u>pan</u> <u>ma</u>, quickly, I need a <u>pan</u> <u>ma</u>! <u>Panama</u> is depicted as the <u>ice</u> <u>cream</u> <u>dripping</u> out the bottom of the sugar cone in our Man and Ice Cream Pictography.

Use Map and Fill in Facts.

Name of Nation_____

Capital_____

Boundaries (Bordering Nations and/or Bodies of Water):

1._____ 2._____ 3._____

   4._____   5._____

Area: 29,761 sq. mi. **Comparative size:** slightly smaller than South Carolina
Terrain: interior mostly steep, rugged mountains; coastal areas largely plains and hills
Climate: tropical maritime; hot, humid, cloudy; prolonged rainy season May-January.
Geographic Note: strategic location on eastern end of isthmus forming land bridge
connecting North and South America; controls Panama Canal that links North Atlantic
Ocean via Caribbean Sea with North Pacific Ocean
Population: 2,882,329 people
Languages: (official) Spanish; English 14%
Religion: Roman Catholic 85%, Protestant 15%
Type of Government: constitutional democracy
Exports: bananas, shrimp, sugar, coffee, clothing
Currency: balboa (PAB); US dollar (USD)

FLAG DESCRIPTION: It is divided into four, equal rectangles; the top
quadrants: white (hoist side) with a blue, five-pointed star in the center and
plain red. The bottom quadrants are plain blue (hoist side) and white with
a red, five-pointed star in the center.

Draw and Color Flag.

Hoist

Fly

Identify the Flags of Man and Ice Cream Pictography.

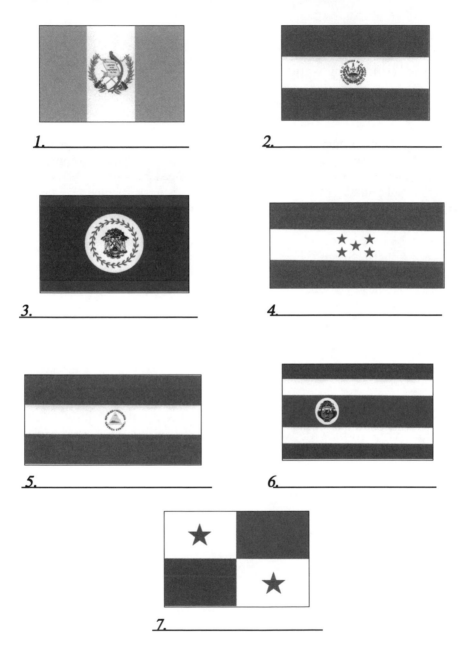

1._____

2._____

3._____

4._____

5._____

6._____

7._____

Identify Nations of Man and Ice Cream Pictography.

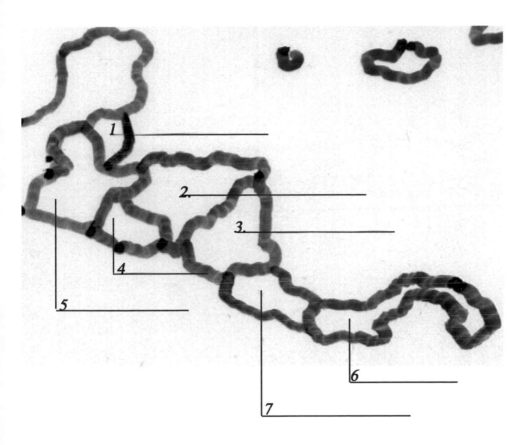

Asia
Rooster Chasing Caterpillar

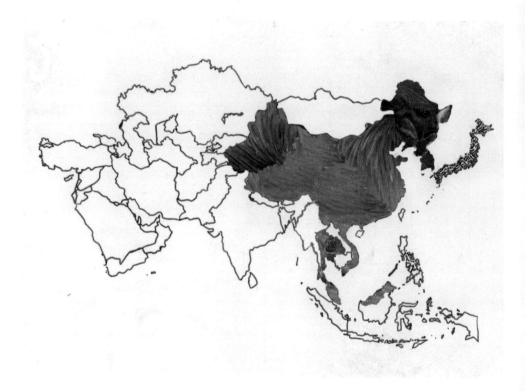

China

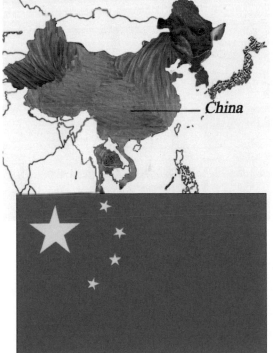

Mnemonic Device: <u>China</u> is depicted as the entire length of the body: <u>from tip of beak, to tail feathers.</u> It does not include wattles, legs, or feet.

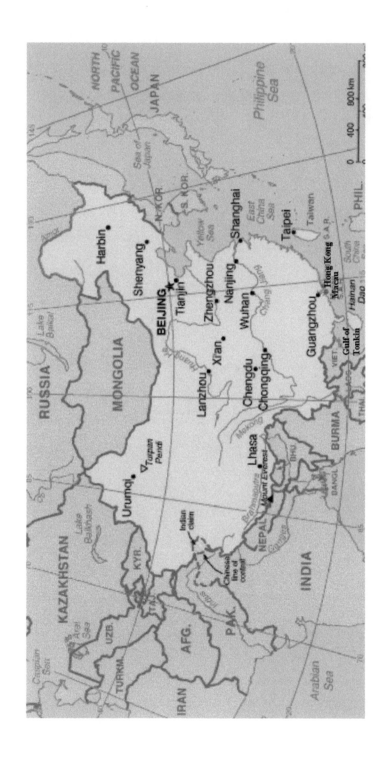

Use Map and Fill in Facts.

Name of Nation_____Capital _____
Land Boundaries:1._____2._____3._____
4._____5._____6._____7._____
8._____9._____10._____11._____
   12._____13._____14._____
   15._____16._____
Bordering Waters: 1._____2._____
   3._____4._____

Area: 3,705,390 sq. mi. **Comparative size:** slightly smaller than the United States
Terrain: mostly mountains, high plateaus, deserts in west; plains, deltas, hills in east
Climate: extremely diverse; tropical in south to subarctic in north
Geographic Note: world's fourth-largest country (after Russia, Canada, and USA),
Mt. Everest on the border with Nepal, is the world's tallest peak; soybean is believed to
have originated in China
Population: 1,284,303,705 people
Languages: Standard Chinese or Mandarin (Putonghua), Yue (Cantonese), Wu
(Shanghaiese), Minbei (Fuzhou), Minnan (Hokkien-Taiwanese), Xiang, Gan
Religion: officially atheist; Christian 3-4%; Daoist (Taoist), Buddhist, Muslim 1-2%
Type of Government: Communist state
Exports: machinery and equipment; textile and clothing, footwear, toys and sporting
goods; mineral fuels
Currency: yuan (CNY)
FLAG DESCRIPTION: It has a red field with a large, yellow, five-
pointed star and four smaller, yellow, five-pointed stars (arranged in a
vertical arc toward the middle of the flag) in the upper hoist-side corner.

Draw and Color Flag.

Hoist   Fly

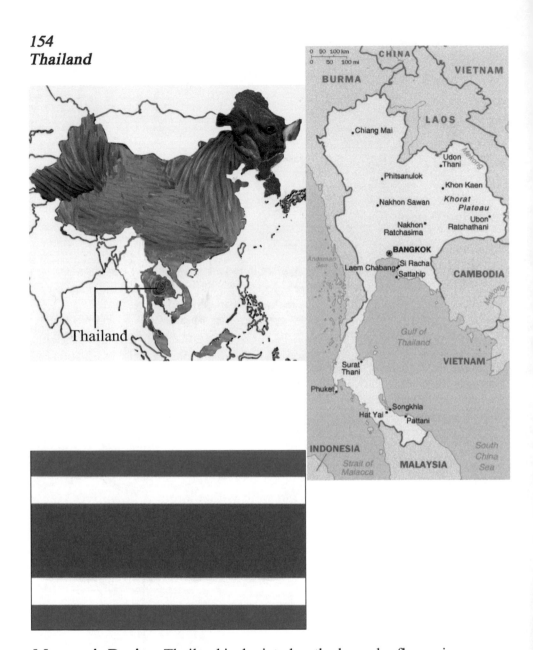

Mnemonic Device: Thailand is depicted as the lavender flower in our Rooster Pictography. This flower is tied around the Rooster's right leg. For fun, let's say that this is the land of ties--where men wearing ties, tie flowers to Roosters.

Use Map and Fill in Facts.

Name of Nation_____
Capital_____
Boundaries (Bordering Nations and/or Bodies of Water):
1._____2._____3._____
4._____5._____6._____

Area: 198,456 sq. mi. **Comparative size:** about twice the size of Wyoming
Terrain: central plain; Khorat Plateau in the east; mountains elsewhere
Climate: tropical; southern isthmus always hot and humid; cloudy southwest monsoon mid-May to September; monsoon season in northeast from November to mid-March
Geographic Note: controls only land route from Asia to Malaysia and Singapore
Population: 62,354,402 people
Languages: Thai, English (secondary language of the elite), ethnic and regional dialects
Religion: Buddhism 95%, Muslim 3.8%, Christianity 0.5%, Hinduism 0.1% other 0.6%
Type of Government: constitutional monarchy
Exports: computers, transistors, seafood, clothing, rice
Currency: baht (THB)

FLAG DESCRIPTION: There are five horizontal bands: red (top), white, blue (double width), white, and red.

Draw and Color Flag.

Hoist   Fly

North Korea

Mnemonic Device: Our Rooster Pictography has a wattle that is divided into an upper section and a lower section. <u>North Korea</u> is depicted as the <u>upper</u> section, or northern section of <u>wattle</u>; it occupies the northern half of the Korean Peninsula.

Use Map and Fill in Facts.

Name of Nation_____
Capital_____
Boundaries (Bordering Nations and/or Bodies of Water):
1._____2._____3._____
          4._____5._____

Area: 46,541 sq. mi. **Comparative size:** about the size of Mississippi
Terrain: mostly hill and mountains separated by deep, narrow valley; coastal plains wide in west, discontinuous in east
Climate: temperate with rainfall concentrated in summer
Geographic Note: strategic location bordering China, South Korea, and Russia; mountainous interior is isolated and sparsely populated
Population:22,224,195 people
Languages: Korean
Religion: traditionally Buddhist and Confucianist, there are some Christian; note: government-sponsored religious groups exist to provide illusion of religious freedom
Type of Government: authoritarian socialist; one-man dictatorship
Exports: minerals, metallurgical products, manufactures (including armaments); textile and fishery products
Currency: North Korean won (KPW)

FLAG DESCRIPTION: There are three horizontal bands: blue (top), red (triple width), and blue. The red band is edged in white. On the hoist-side of the red band, is a white disk with a red, five-pointed star.

Draw and Color Flag.

Hoist

Fly

Mnemonic Device: <u>South Korea</u> occupies the southern half of the Korean Peninsula. It is depicted as the <u>lower,</u> or southern <u>wattle</u> of our Rooster Pictography.

Use Map and Fill in Facts.

Name of Nation_____
Capital_____
Boundaries (Bordering Nations and/or Bodies of Water):
1._____2._____3._____

Area: 38,023 sq. mi. **Comparative size:** about the size of Indiana
Terrain: mostly hill and mountains; wide coastal plains in west and south
Climate: temperate with rainfall concentrated in summer
Geographic Note: strategic location on Korea Strait
Population: 48,324,000 people
Languages: Korean; English widely taught in junior high and high school
Religion: Christian 49%. Buddhist 47%, Confucianist 3%, other 1%
Type of Government: republic
Exports: electronic products, machinery and equipment, motor vehicles, steel, ships; textiles, clothing, footwear; fish
Currency: South Korean won (KRW)

FLAG DESCRIPTION: It has a white field with a red (top) and blue, yin-yang symbol in the center. There is a different black trigram from the ancient I Ching (Book of Changes) in each corner of the white field.

Draw and Color Flag.

Hoist

Fly

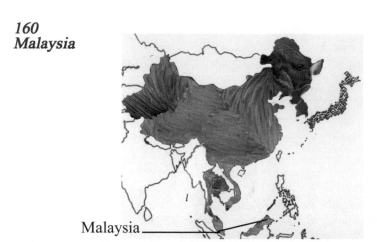

Malaysia _____

Mnemonic Device: Malaysia is comprised of two distinct landmasses: the southern part of the Malay peninsula, and Sarawak and Sabah in northern Borneo. <u>Malaysia</u> is depicted as the <u>extended</u> <u>foot</u>, and similarly colored <u>ground</u> in our Rooster Pictography.

Use Map and Fill in Facts.

Name of Nation_____
Capital_____
Boundaries (Bordering Nations and/or Bodies of Water):
1._____2._____3._____
4._____5._____6._____
　　7._____8._____

Area: 128,400 sq. mi. **Comparative size:** about the size of New Mexico
Terrain: coastal plains rising to hills and mountains
Climate: tropical; annual monsoons southwest from April to October; northwest monsoons from October to February
Geographic Note: strategic location along Strait of Malacca and Southern China Sea
Population: 22,662,365 people
Languages: (official) Bahasa Melayu; English, Chinese dialects, Tamil, Telugu, Malayalam, Panjabi; east Malaysia: Iban and Kadazan
Religion: Muslim Buddhist, Daoist, Hindu, Christian, Sikh; East Malaysia Shamanism
Type of Government: constitutional monarchy
Exports: electronic equipment, petroleum and liquified natural gas, wood and wood products, palm oil, rubber, textiles, chemicals
Currency: ringgit (MYR)

FLAG DESCRIPTION: There are 14 equal horizontal stripes: red (top) alternating with white (bottom). There is a blue rectangle in the upper, hoist-side corner bearing a yellow crescent, and a yellow, fourteen-pointed star. The crescent and the star are traditional symbols of Islam, but the design was based on the flag of the United States.

Draw and Color Flag.

Hoist　　　　　　　　　　　　　　Fly

Mnemonic Device: Vietnam is located on the eastern side of the Indochinese Peninsula. It lies between two major river systems. It is depicted as the <u>retracted leg</u> of our Rooster Pictography. The top of this leg starts out in the shape of a <u>V</u> for <u>Vietnam</u>. It then comes down and around to help him run quickly.

Use Map and Fill in Facts.

Name of Nation_____
Capital_____
Boundaries (Bordering Nations and/or Bodies of Water):
1._____ 2._____ 3._____
　　4._____ 5._____

Area: 129,806 sq. mi. **Comparative size:** about the size of New Mexico
Terrain: low, flat delta in south and north; central highlands; hilly, mountainous in far north and northwest
Climate: tropical in south; monsoons in north mid-May to Mid-September
Geographic Note: this country is only about 30 miles across at its narrowest point
Population: 81,098,416 people
Languages: (official) Vietnamese; English; some French,Chinese, and Khmer
Religion: Buddhist, Hoa Hao, Cao Dai, Christian, indigenous beliefs, Muslim
Type of Government: Communist state
Exports: crude oil, marine products, rice, coffee, rubber, tea, garments, shoes
Currency: dong (VND)

FLAG DESCRIPTION: It has a red field with a large, yellow, five-pointed star in the center.

Draw and Color Flag.

Hoist

Fly

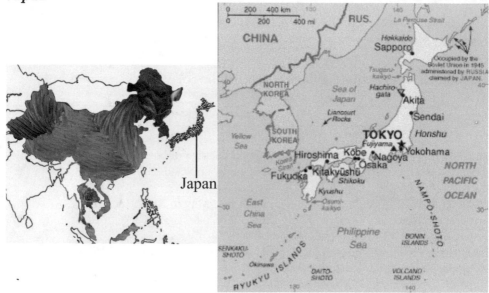

Mnemonic Device: About 98% of Japan's territory is made up of four islands that are so close in proximity, that they are physically connected via tunnels and bridges. In our Rooster Pictography, <u>Japan</u> is depicted as the <u>caterpillar</u> which the Rooster would like to have for a meal. However, Japan stays out of the frying pan! The sun device of Japan's flag is like a red, hot frying pan.

Use Map and Fill in Facts.

Name of Nation_____
Capital_____
Boundaries (Bordering Nations and/or Bodies of Water):
1._____ 2._____ 3._____
4._____ 5._____ 6._____

Area: 143,749 sq. mi. **Comparative size:** about the size of California
Terrain: mostly rugged and mountainous
Climate: tropical in south; cool temperate in north
Geographic Note: strategic location in northeast Asia
Population: 126,974,628 people
Languages: Japanese
Religion: Shinto and Buddhist 84%; other 16% (includes Christian 0.7%)
Type of Government: constitutional monarchy with a parliamentary government
Exports: motor vehicles, semiconductors, office machinery, chemicals
Currency: yen (JPY)

FLAG DESCRIPTION: It has a white field with a large, red disk (representing the sun without rays) in the center.

Draw and Color Flag.

Hoist

Fly

Identify the Flags of Rooster Pictography.

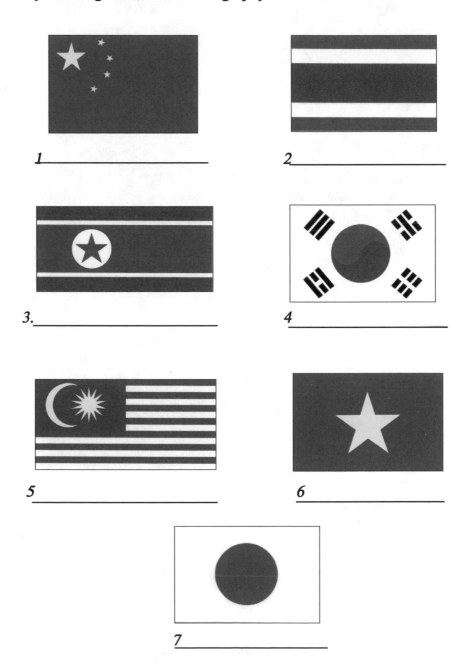

1 _____

2 _____

3. _____

4 _____

5 _____

6 _____

7 _____

Identify Nations of Rooster Pictography.

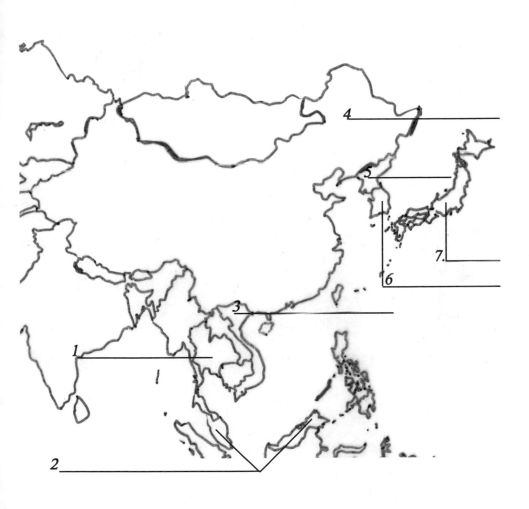

<u>Asia</u> *Butterfly*   *Azerbaijan*

Mnemonic Device: <u>Azer</u>baijan is depicted as a <u>butterfly</u>--a boy butterfly named John. It is perched on the banks of the Caspian Sea. Imagine Azerbijian's flag flittering around the room. Now picture John, the butterfly, flittering and flying right out the window. Wave to him while saying, "Azer BYE John."

Use Map and Fill in Facts.

Name of Nation_____
Capital_____
Boundaries (Bordering Nations and/or Bodies of Water):
1._____2._____3._____
4._____ Naxcivan exclave 5._____

Area: 33,400 sq. mi. **Comparative size:** about the size of Maine
Terrain: large, flat Kura-Araks Lowland; Caucasus Mountains to the north, Baku lies on Apsheron Peninsula that juts into Caspian Sea
Climate: dry, semiarid
Geographic Note: both the main area of the country and the Naxcivan exclave are landlocked
Population: 7,798,497 people
Languages: Azerbaijani (Azeri) 89%, Russian 3%, Armenian 2%, other 6%
Religion: Muslim 93.4%, Russian Orthodox 2.5%, Armenian Orthodox 2.3% other 1.8%
Type of Government: republic
Exports: oil and gas 90%, machinery, cotton, foodstuffs
Currency: Azerbaijani manat (AZM)

FLAG DESCRIPTION: There are three equal horizontal bands: blue (top), red, and green; a crescent and eight-pointed star in white are centered in red band.

Draw and Color Flag.

Hoist

Fly

Asia *Arrow*   *Uzbekistan*

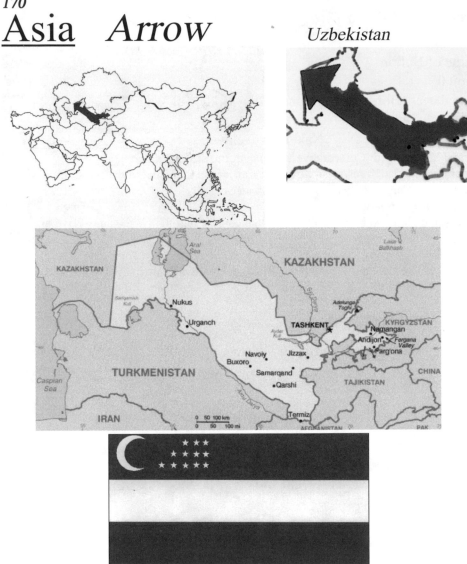

Mnemonic Device: <u>Uzbekistan</u>'s sharp, <u>arrow</u> head extends into the Aral Sea; the vanes at its end reach to the Pamirs-a mountainous region. Let's pretend the arrow's sharp, pointed head cuts your arm. You then put a white bandage on the cut, but your blood still <u>oozes</u> out the edges of the bandage. The flag's white stripe edged in red looks like a bandage, with blood <u>ooz</u>ing out of it.--/<u>Ooze</u> beck i stan/.

Use Map and Fill in Facts.

Name of Nation_____
Capital_____
Boundaries (Bordering Nations and/or Bodies of Water):
1._____ 2._____ 3._____
    4._____ 5._____
Area: 172,700 sq. mi. **Comparative size:** about the size of California
Terrain: mostly sandy desert with dunes; intensely irrigated river valleys along course of Amu Darya; shrinking Aral Sea in west
Climate: long, hot summers; mild winters
Geographic Note: along with Liechtenstein, one of the only two doubly landlocked countries in the world
Population: 25,563,441 people
Languages: Uzbek 74.3%, Russian 14.2%, Tajik 4.4%, other 7.1%
Religion: Muslim 88% (mostly Sunnis), Eastern Orthodox 9%, other 3%
Type of Government: republic; authoritarian presidential rule, with little power outside the executive branch
Exports: cotton 41.5%, gold 9.6%, energy products 9.6%, mineral fertilizers, ferrous metals, textiles, food products, automoblies
Currency: Uzbekistani sum (UZS)

FLAG DESCRIPTION: There are three equal horizontal bands: blue (top), white, edged in red, and green. It has a white, crescent moon and 12 white stars in the upper hoist-side quadrant.

Draw and Color Flag.

Hoist

Fly

Identify Flags of Butterfly and Arrow Pictographies.

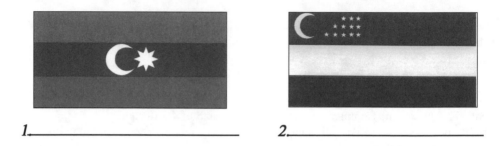

1._____   2._____

Identify Nations of Butterfly and Arrow Pictographies.

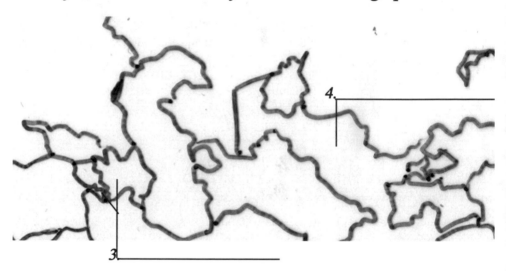

Asia

Ballerina

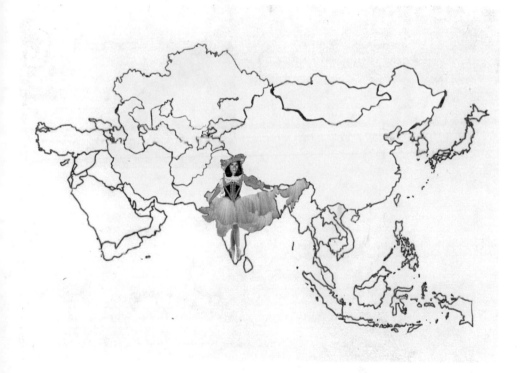

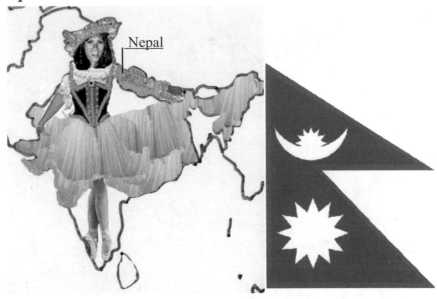

Nepal

Mnemonic Device: <u>Nepal</u> is depicted as the Ballerina's <u>left arm</u> which is covered in a pink, pearled sleeve. Nepal's flag is unique in shape. In fact, its shape reminds us of the mighty, jagged mountain range of the Himalayas that are at the heart of Nepal. This is where we find Mt. Everest, the highest mountain peak in the world.

Use Map and Fill in Facts.

Name of Nation_____

Capital_____

Boundaries (Bordering Nations and/or Bodies of Water):

     1._____2._____

Area: 56,827 sq. mi. **Comparative size:** about the size of Arkansas

Terrain: Flat river plain of the Ganges in south, central hill region, rugged Himalayas in north

Climate: varies from cool summers and severe winters in north to subtropical summers and mild winters in south

Geographic Note: landlocked; strategic location between China and India; contains eight of world's 10 highest peaks, including Mt. Everest -world's tallest- borders China

Population: 25,873,917 people

Languages: Nepali (official, spoken by 90%), about a dozen other languages and about 30 major dialects

Religion: Hinduism 86.2%, Buddhism 7.8%, Islam 3.8%, other 2.2%

Type of Government: parliamentary democracy and constitutional monarchy

Exports: carpets, clothing, leather goods, jute goods, grain

Currency: Nepalese rupee (NPR)

FLAG DESCRIPTION: It has a red field with a blue border around the unique shape of two overlapping right triangles. The smaller, upper triangle bears a white stylized moon, and the larger, lower triangle bears a white 12-pointed sun.

Draw and Color Flag.

Hoist

Fly

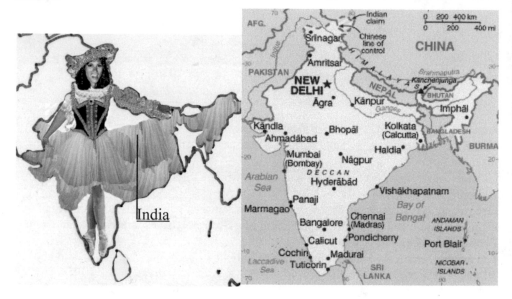

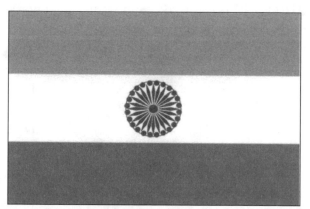

Mnemonic Device: The central device is a *chakra (wheel)* from the capital of the ancient Asokan column. Just as the wheel spins and whirls around and around, so too does our Ballerina Pictography. India is depicted as all of the ballerina, except for her left arm.

Use Map and Fill in Facts.

Name of Nation_____

Capital_____

Boundaries (Bordering Nations and/or Bodies of Water):

1._____ 2._____ 3._____

4._____ 5._____ 6._____

    7._____ 8._____

Area: 1,269,340 sq. mi. **Comparative size:** slightly more than one-third size of USA
Terrain: upland plain in south; flat to rolling plain along the Ganges; deserts in west;
Himalayas in north
Climate: tropical monsoons in south; temperate in north
Geographic Note: dominates South Asian subcontinent; near important Indian Ocean
trade routes
Population: 1,045,845,226 people
Languages: English most important for national, political, and commercial communi-
cation; Hindi is the national language and primary tongue of 30%; there are 14 other
official languages, e.g., Bengali, Teluga, Marathi, Tamil, Urdu, Gujarati
Religion: Hindu 81.3%; Muslim 12%; Christian 2.3%, Sikh 1.9%, other groups
including Buddhist, Jain, Parsi 2.5%
Type of Government: federal republic
Exports: textile goods, gems and jewelry, engineering goods, chemicals, leather
manufactures
Currency: Indian rupee (INR)

FLAG DESCRIPTION: There are three equal horizontal bands: orange
(top), white, and green with a blue chakra (24-spoked wheel) centered in
the white band.

Draw and Color Flag.

Hoist

Fly

Asia *Stan the Duck with Afghan*   *Pakistan*

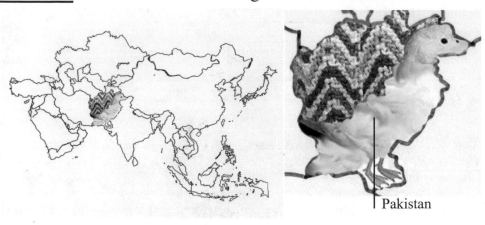

Pakistan

Mnemonic Device: In this part of the world, we notice many "Stans." Our Duck Pictography is also named Stan. He always packs the afghan his mommy knitted him when he was just an egg; he never needs to be reminded to "<u>Pack</u> <u>it</u> <u>Stan</u>." <u>Pakistan</u> is depicted as the <u>duck</u>.

Use Map and Fill in Facts.

Name of Nation_____
Capital_____
Boundaries (Bordering Nations and/or Bodies of Water):
1._____2._____3._____
        4._____ 5._____

Area: 310,402 sq. mi. **Comparative size:** slightly less than twice the size of California
Terrain: flat Indus plain in east; mountains in north and northwest.
Climate: mostly hot, dry desert; temperate in northwest; arctic in north
Geographic Note: traditional invasion routes between Central Asia and the Indian Subcontinent
Population: 147,663,429 people
Languages: (official) Urdu, English; Punjabi, Sindhi, Siraiki (a Punjabi variant), Pashtu, Balochi, Hindko, Brahui, Burushaski, and others
Religion: Muslim 97% (Sunni 77%, Shi'a 20%), Christian, Hindu, and other 3%
Type of Government: federal republic
Exports: textiles (garments, cotton, cloth, and yarn), rice, other agricultural products
Currency: Pakistani rupee (PKR)

FLAG DESCRIPTION: It has a green field with a vertical white band symbolizing the role of religious minorities on the hoist side. A large, white crescent and star are centered in the green field. The crescent, star, and color green are traditional symbols of Islam.

Draw and Color Flag:

Hoist   Fly

Afghanistan

Afghanistan

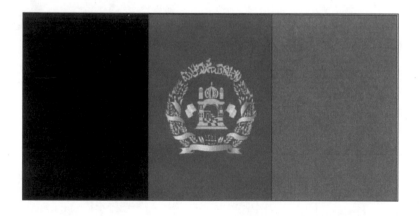

Mnemonic Device: <u>Afghanistan</u> is depicted as the <u>afghan</u> of our Stan the Duck Pictography.

Use Map and Fill in Facts.

Name of Nation_____
Capital_____
Boundaries (Bordering Nations and/or Bodies of Water):
1._____2._____3._____
4._____5._____6._____

Area: 250,000 sq. mi. **Comparative size:** slightly smaller than Texas
Terrain: mostly rugged mountains; plains in north and southwest
Climate: arid to semiarid; cold winters and hot summers
Geographic Note: landlocked; the Hindu Kush mountains that run northeast to south-west divide the northern provinces from the rest of the country
Population: 27,755,775 people
Languages: Afghan Persian, Pashtu, Turkic languages (Uzbek and Turkmen)
Religion: Sunni Muslim 84%, Shi'a Muslim 15%, other 1%
Type of Government: transitional
Exports: opium, fruit and nuts, handwoven carpets, wool, cotton, hides and pelts, precious and semi-precious gems
Currency: afghani (AFA)

FLAG DESCRIPTION: There are three equal vertical bands: black (hoist), red, and green. There is a gold emblem centered on the red band. The emblem features a temple-like structure encircled by a wreath on the left and right and by a bold Islamic inscription above.

Draw and Color Flag.

Hoist

Fly

Identify Flags of Ballerina and Duck Pictographies.

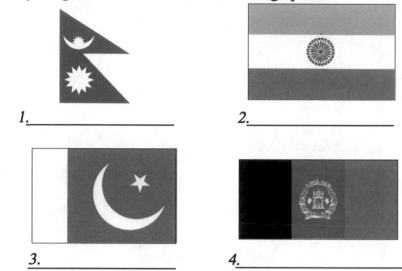

1._____ 2._____

3._____ 4._____

Identify Nations of Ballerina and Duck Pictographies.

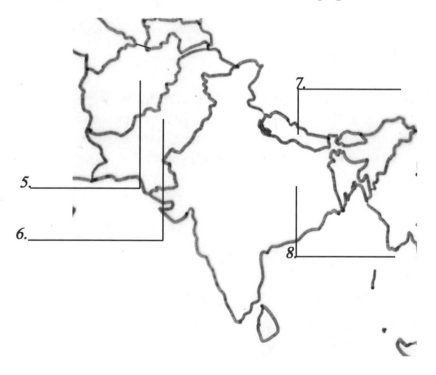

<u>Asia</u>
Man Wearing Bow Tie

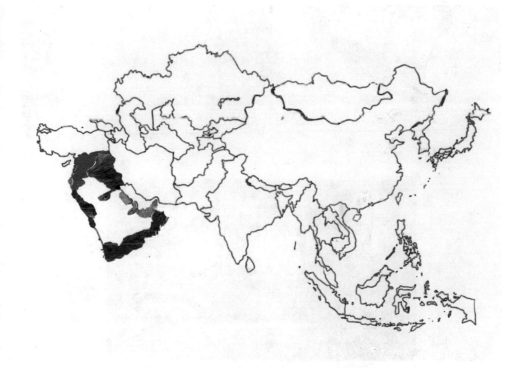

Mnemonic Device: Saudi Arabia occupies most of the Arabian Peninsula. It houses Mecca--Muhammad's birthplace, Medina (where the religion of Islam began), and one-quarter of the world's petroleum reserves. So today, let's meet a man whose nickname is naughty, first name is Saudi, and last name is Arabia. <u>Saudi</u> <u>Arabia</u> is depicted as the <u>face</u> (including ear) of our Man Wearing Bow Tie Pictography.

Use Map and Fill in Facts.

Name of Nation_____
Capital_____
Boundaries (Bordering Nations and/or Bodies of Water):
1._____ 2._____ 3._____ 4._____
5._____ 6._____ 7._____ 8._____
            9._____ 10._____

Area: 829,996 sq. mi. **Comparative size:** about one-fifth the size of USA
Terrain: mostly uninhabited, sandy desert
Climate: harsh, dry desert with great temperature extremes
Geographic Note: extensive coastines on Persian Gulf and Red Sea provide great
leverage on shipping (especially crude oil) through Persian Gulf and Suez Canal
Population: 23,513,330 people
Languages: Arabic
Religion: Muslim 100%
Type of Government: monarchy
Exports: petroleum and petroleum products 90%
Currency: Saudi riyal (SAR)

FLAG DESCRIPTION: It has a green field with large white Arabic
script (that may be translated as "There is no God but God; Muhammad is
the Messenger of God" above a white horizontal saber (the tip points to
the hoist side). Green is the traditional color of Islam.

Draw and Color Flag.

Hoist   Fly

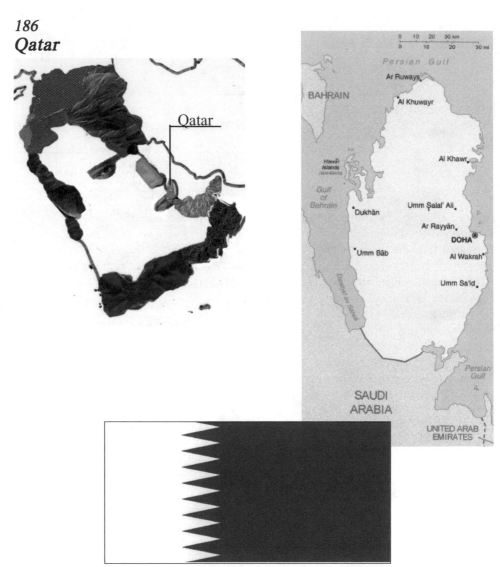

Mnemonic Device: Qatar is a wealthy emirate in the Persian Gulf who, in 1971, choose not to belong to the U.A.E., as a member state, but rather to be independent. Qatar is depicted as the tongue in our Man Wearing Bow Tie Pictography. Now I hear that naughty, Saudi Arabia bought a guitar from Qatar. You could ask him yourself if this is so, but I don't think he will answer you, at least not while he is sticking his tongue out like that! What's the matter? Qatar (Cat-ar) got your tongue?

Use Map and Fill in Facts.

Name of Nation_____

Capital_____

Boundaries (Bordering Nations and/or Bodies of Water):

1._____2._____3._____

Area: 4,427 sq. mi. **Comparative size:** about the size of Connecticut

Terrain: mostly flat and barren desert covered with loose sand and gravel

Climate: arid; mild, pleasant winters; very hot, humid summers

Geographic Note: strategic location in central Persian Gulf near major petroleum deposits

Population: 793,341 people

Languages: (official) Arabic; English commonly used as a second language

Religion: Muslim 95%

Type of Government: traditional monarchy

Exports: petroleum products 80%, fertilizers, steel

Currency: Qatari rial (QAR)

FLAG DESCRIPTION: It is maroon with a broad, white, serrated band (nine, white points) on the hoist side.

Draw and Color Flag.

Hoist   Fly

Iraq

Mnemonic Device: Naughty Saudi Arabia has been racking his brain to learn how to play the guitar he bought from Qatar. When he racks his brain it looks something like this: place palm of hand about an inch away from forehead. Nod head so that palm makes contact with forehead while head is moving forward, but not while head is moving backwards. Saudi wears a <u>big bang</u> on his forehead; this is where his palm hits when he says, "<u>I rack,</u> I rack, I rack my brain! <u>Iraq</u> is depicted as the <u>big bang</u> of our Man Wearing Bow Tie Pictography.

Use Map and Fill in Facts.

Name of Nation_____
Capital_____
Boundaries (Bordering Nations and/or Bodies of Water):
1._____2._____3._____
4._____5._____6._____

Area: 167,923 sq. mi. **Comparative size:** about twice the size of Idaho
Terrain: mostly broad plains; reedy marshes along Iranian border in south with large flooded areas; mountains along borders with Iran and Turkey
Climate: mostly desert; mild to cool winters; dry, hot cloudless summers
Geographic Note: strategic location on Shatt al Arab waterway and at the head of the Persian Gulf
Population: 24,001,816 people
Languages. (official) Arabic, Kurdish (official in some regions); Assyrian, Armenian
Religion: Muslim 97% (Shi'a 60-65%, Sunni 32-37%) Christian or other 3%
Type of Government: transitional government
Exports: crude oil
Currency: Iraqi dinar (IQD)

FLAG DESCRIPTION: There are three equal horizontal bands: red (top), white, and black with three, green, five-pointed stars in a horizontal line centered in the white band. The phrase ALLAHU AKBAR (God is Great) is in green Arabic script.--Allahu to the right of the middle star, and Akbar to the left of the middle star-- was added in January 1991 during the Persian Gulf crisis.

Draw and Color Flag.

Hoist   Fly

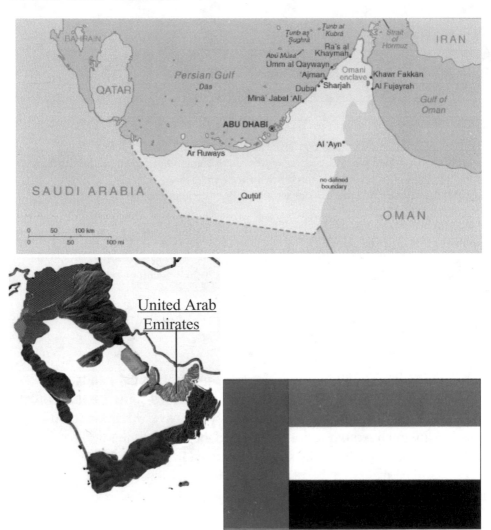

Mnemonic Device: In 1971 seven small principalities became independent from their British protectorate to form the federation of sheikdoms--now know as the United Arab Emirates (UAE, listen to CD jingle). In our Man Wearing Bow Tie Pictography, we see that the man's beard grows in two different colors. The UAE is depicted as the lighter colored beard located closest to Saudi's mouth.

Use Map and Fill in Facts.

Name of Nation_____
Capital_____
Boundaries (Bordering Nations and/or Bodies of Water):
    1._____2._____
    3._____4._____

Area: 32,276 sq. mi. **Comparative size:** slightly smaller than Maine
Terrain: barren coastal plain; sand dunes of vast desert wasteland; mountains in east
Climate: desert; cooler in eastern mountains
Geographic Note: strategic location along southern approaches to Strait of Hormuz, a
vital transit point for world crude oil
Population: 2,445,989 people
Languages: (official) Arabic; Persian, English, Hindi, Urdu
Religion: Muslim 96% (Shi'a 16%) Christian, Hindu, and other 4%
Type of Government: federation with specified powers delegated to the UAE federal
government and other powers reserved to member emirates
Exports: crude oil 45%, natural gas, reexports, dried fish, dates
Currency: Emirati dirham (AED)

FLAG DESCRIPTION: There are three equal horizontal bands: green
(top), white, and black with a wider red vertical band on the hoist side.

Draw and Color Flag.

Hoist   Fly

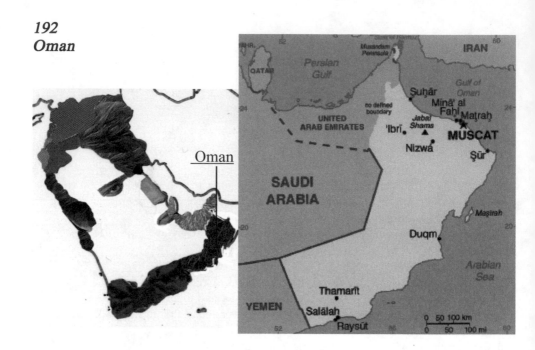

Oman

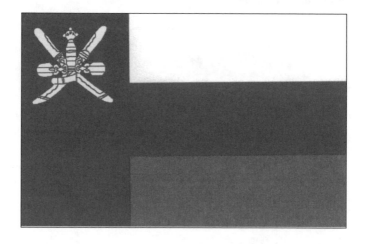

Mnemonic Device: Neither a lady nor a child can grow a beard; only a
<u>man </u> can grow a beard. <u>Oman</u> is depicted as the <u>dark-colored beard</u> of our
Man Wearing a Bow Tie Pictography. Listen to CD jingle of "Oh Man... I
say, Yea Man."

Use Map and Fill in Facts.

Name of Nation_____
Capital_____
Boundaries (Bordering Nations and/or Bodies of Water):
    1._____2._____
    3._____4._____

Area: 82,025 sq. mi. **Comparative size:** slightly smaller than Kansas
Terrain: central desert plain, rugged mountains in north and south
Climate: hot, dry desert interior; humid along coast; strong southwest summer monsoon from May to September in far south
Geographic Note: strategic location on Musandam Peninsula adjacent to Strait of Hormuz, a vital transit point for world crude oil
Population: 2,713,462 people
Languages: (official) Arabic; English, Baluchi, Urdu, Indian dialects
Religion: Ibadhi Muslim 75%, Sunni Muslim Shi'a Muslim, Hindu
Type of Government: monarchy
Exports: petroleum, reexports, fish, metals, textiles
Currency: Omani rial (OMR)

FLAG DESCRIPTION: There are three equal horizontal bands: white (top), red, and green. There is a broad, vertical, red band on the hoist side. The national emblem (a khanjar dagger in its sheath superimposed on two crossed swords in scabbards) in white, is centered at the top of the vertical band.

Draw and Color Flag.

Hoist   Fly

Yemen

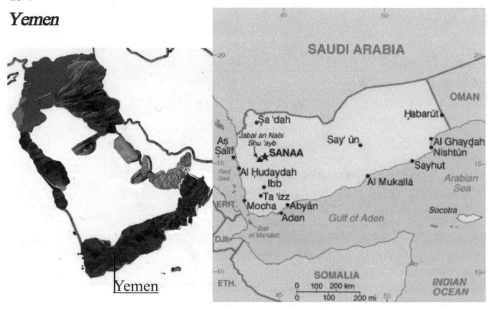

Yemen

Mnemonic Device: Yemen is located on the southwest corner of the Arabian Peninsula. <u>Yemen</u> is depicted as the <u>bow tie </u>of our Man Wearing Bow Tie Pictography. Listen to CD jingle of "Oh Man,...I say, Yea Man."

Use Map and Fill in Facts.

Name of Nation_____

Capital_____

Boundaries (Bordering Nations and/or Bodies of Water):

1._____2._____3._____

    4._____5._____

Area: 203,849 sq. mi. **Comparative size:** about twice the size of Wyoming

Terrain: narrow coastal plain backed by hills and rugged mountains; desert interior

Climate: hot and humid along west coast; extraordinarily hot, dry, harsh desert in east

Geographic Note: strategic location on Bab el Mandeb, the strait linking the Red Sea and the Gulf of Aden, one of the world's most active shipping lanes

Population: 18,701,257 people

Languages: Arabic

Religion: Muslim including Shaf'i (Sunni) and Zaydi (Shi'a), small numbers of Jewish, Christian, and Hindu

Type of Government: republic

Exports: crude oil, coffee, dried and salted fish

Currency: Yemeni rial (YER)

FLAG DESCRIPTION: There are three equal horizontal bands: red (top), white, and black.

Draw and Color Flag.

Hoist   Fly

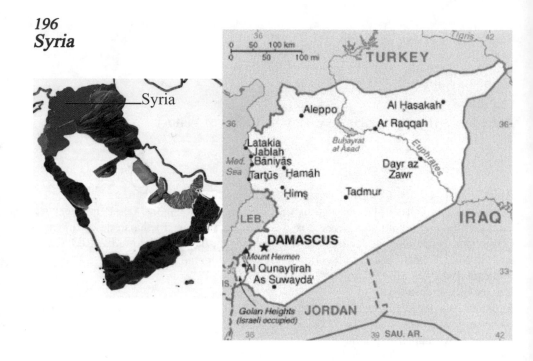

Mnemonic Device: The sun is <u>searing</u> the top of the man's head. For this reason he is wearing a cap; the <u>top, red part of his cap</u> is searing... <u>Syria</u>; Syria's flag, like the man, is capped in red.

Use Map and Fill in Facts.

Name of Nation_____
Capital_____
Boundaries (Bordering Nations and/or Bodies of Water):
1._____2._____3._____
4._____5._____6._____

Area: 71,499 sq. mi. **Comparative size:** about the size of North Dakota
Terrain: semiarid and desert plateau; narrow coastal plain; mountains in west
Climate: hot, dry, sunny summers (June to August) and mild, rainy winters along coast
Geographic Note: there are 42 Israeli settlements and civilian land use sites in the Israeli-occupied Golan Heights
Population: 17,155,814 people
Languages: (official) Arabic; Kurdish, Armenian, Aramaic
Religion: Sunni Muslim 74%, Alawite, Druze, and other Muslim sects 16%, Christian 10%, Jewish (tiny communities in Damascus, Al Qamishli, and Aleppo)
Type of Government: republic under military regime since March 1963
Exports: crude oil 68%; textile 7%, fruits and vegetables 6%, raw cotton 4%
Currency: Syrian pound (SYP)

FLAG DESCRIPTION: There are three equal horizontal bands: red (top), white, and black with two small green, five-pointed stars in a horizontal line centered in the white band.

Draw and Color Flag.

Hoist

Fly

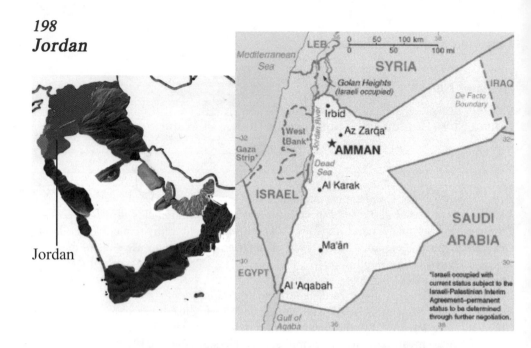

Jordan

Mnemonic Device: Jordan's flag was introduced when learning about Sudan. These nations are linked by the "Jordan, Sudan, Ol'Dan Tucker" jingle. Also, since Jordan is always having dinner with Sudan, and since their flags look similar, imagine that Jordan is Sudan's "cousin" who lives across the Red Sea. The <u>Red</u> Sea will help you remember that Jordan's flag is the one with the <u>red</u> triangle, not the green triangle of Sudan's flag. <u>Jordan</u> is depicted as the <u>side of the cap</u> of our Man Wearing Bow Tie Pictography.

Use Map and Fill in Facts.

Name of Nation_____
Capital_____
Boundaries (Bordering Nations and/or Bodies of Water):
1._____2._____3._____
        4._____5._____

Area: 35,267 sq. mi. **Comparative size:** about the size of Indiana
Terrain: desert in east; highland area in west; Great Rift Valley separates East and West Banks of the Jordan River
Climate: mostly arid desert; rainy season in west (November to April)
Geographic Note: strategic location at the head of the Gulf of Aqaba and as the Arab country that shares the longest border with Israel and the occupied West Bank
Population: 5,307,470 people
Languages: (official) Arabic; English widely understood (upper and middle classes)
Religion: Sunni Muslim 92%, Christian 6%, other 2%
Type of Government: constitutional monarchy
Exports: phosphates, fertilizers, potash, agricultural products, manufactures, pharmaceuticals
Currency: Jordanian dinar (JOD)

FLAG DESCRIPTION: There are three equal horizontal bands: black (top, the Abbassid Caliphate of Islam), white (the Ummayyad Caliphate of Islam), and green (the Fatimid Caliphate of Islam). It has a red isosceles triangle (representing the Great Arab Revolt of 1916) based on the hoist side bearing a small, white, seven-pointed star. This star symbolizes the seven verses of the opening Sura (Al-Fatiha) of the Koran; the seven points represent faith in One God, humanity, national spirit, humility, social justice, virtue, and aspirations.

Draw and Color Flag.

Hoist   Fly

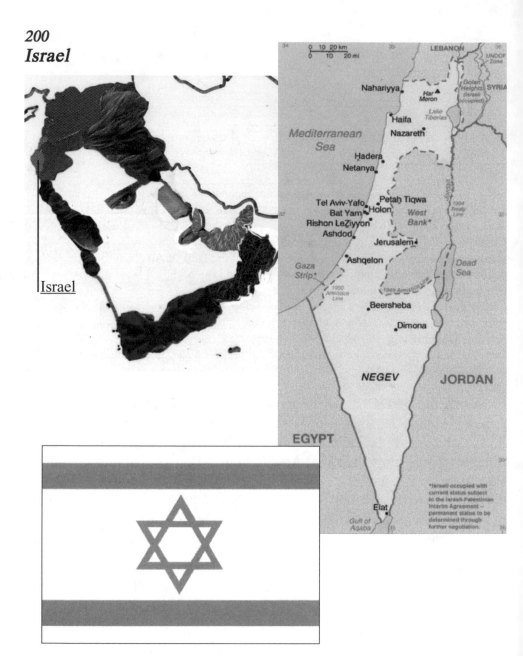

Israel

Mnemonic Device: The Jewish homeland, <u>Israel</u>, is depicted as the blue, <u>back of the cap</u> in our Man Wearing Bow Tie Pictography.
IT <u>IS REAL</u>-- <u>ISRAEL</u>.

Use Map and Fill in Facts.

Name of Nation_____

Capital_____

Boundaries (Bordering Nations and/or Bodies of Water):

1._____ 2._____ 3._____

4._____ 5._____ 6._____

Area: 8,019 sq. mi. **Comparative size:** slightly smaller than New Jersey
Terrain: Negev desert in the south; low coastal plain; central mountains; Jordan Rift Valley
Climate: temperate; hot and dry in southern and eastern desert areas
Geographic Note: There are 231 Israeli settlements and civilian land use sites in the West Bank, 42 in the Israeli-occupied Golan Heights, 25 in the Gaza Strip, and 29 in East Jerusalem. The Sea of Galilee is an important freshwater source.
Population: 6,029,529 people
Languages: (official) Hebrew; Arabic used officially for Arab minority, English most commonly used foreign language
Religion: Jewish 80.1%; Sunni Muslim 14.6%, Christian 2.1%, other 3.2%
Type of Government: parliamentary democracy
Exports: machinery and equipment, software, cut diamonds, agricultural products, chemicals, textiles and apparel
Currency: new Israeli shekel (ILS)

FLAG DESCRIPTION: It has a white field with a blue hexagram (six-pointed linear star) known as the Magen David (Shield of David). This blue hexagram is centered between two equal horizontal blue bands near the top and bottom edges.

Draw and Color Flag.

Hoist   Fly

Lebanon

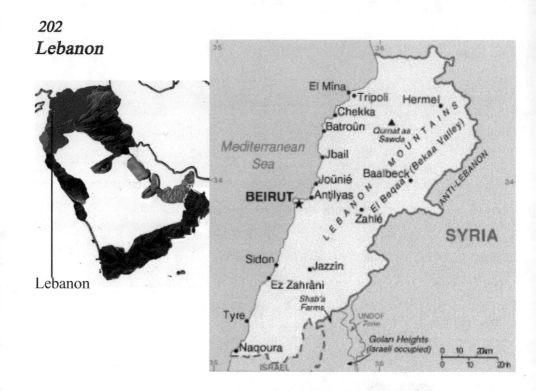

Lebanon

Mnemonic Device: Leban-on-and-on-and-on-and-on... Lebanon is depicted as the brown-colored button found on the back of the cap of our Man Wearing Bow Tie Pictography.

Use Map and Fill in Facts.

Name of Nation_____
Capital_____
Boundaries (Bordering Nations and/or Bodies of Water):
1._____ 2._____ 3._____

Area: 4,015 sq. mi. **Comparative size:** about 0.7 times the size of Connecticut
Terrain: Narrow coastal plain; Bekaa Valley separates Lebanon and Anti-Lebanon Mountains
Climate: Mediterranean; mild to cool, wet winters with hot, dry summers; Lebanon mountains experience heavy winter snows
Geographic Note: Nahr el Litani only major river in Near East not crossing an international boundary; rugged terrain historically helped isolate, protect, and develop numerous factional groups based on religion, clan, and ethnicity
Population: 3,677,780 people
Languages: (official) Arabic; French, English, Armenian
Religion: Muslim 70%; Christian 30%
Type of Government: republic
Exports: foodstuffs and tobacco, textiles, chemicals, precious stones, metal and metal products, electrical equipment and products, jewelry, paper and paper products
Currency: Lebanese pound (LBP)

FLAG DESCRIPTION: It has three horizontal bands of red (top), white (double width), and red with a green cedar tree centered in the white band.

Draw and Color Flag.

Hoist

Fly

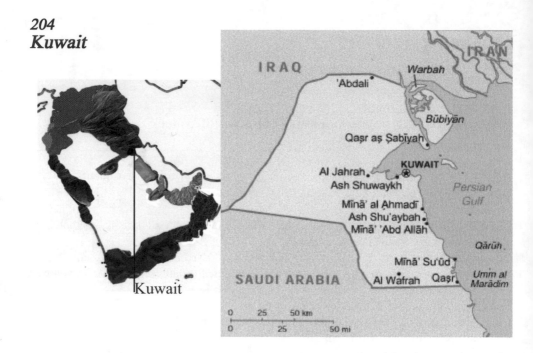

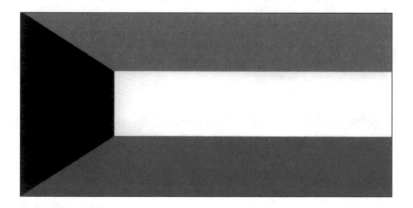

Mnemonic Device: Kuwait is an Arab emirate located in the northwest corner of the Persian Gulf. <u>Kuwait</u> is depicted as a <u>black spot</u> just below the bangs (Iraq) of our Man Wearing Bow Tie Pictography. We say, "wait, wait, Kuwait!

Use Map and Fill in Facts.

Name of Nation_____
Capital_____
Boundaries (Bordering Nations and/or Bodies of Water):
1._____ 2._____ 3._____

Area: 6,880 sq. mi. **Comparative size:** slightly smaller than New Jersey
Terrain: desert plains
Climate: dry desert; intensely hot summers; short, cool winters
Geographic Note: strategic location at the head of Persian Gulf
Population: 2,111,561 people
Languages: (official) Arabic; English widely spoken
Religion: Muslim 85%; Christian, Hindu, Parsi, and other 15%
Type of Government: nominal constitutional monarchy
Exports: oil and refined products, fertilizers
Currency: Kuwaiti dinar (KD)

FLAG DESCRIPTION: There are three equal horizontal bands: green (top), white, and red. A black trapezoid is based on the hoist side.

Draw and Color Flag

Hoist   Fly

Identify Flags of Man Wearing Bow Tie Pictography.

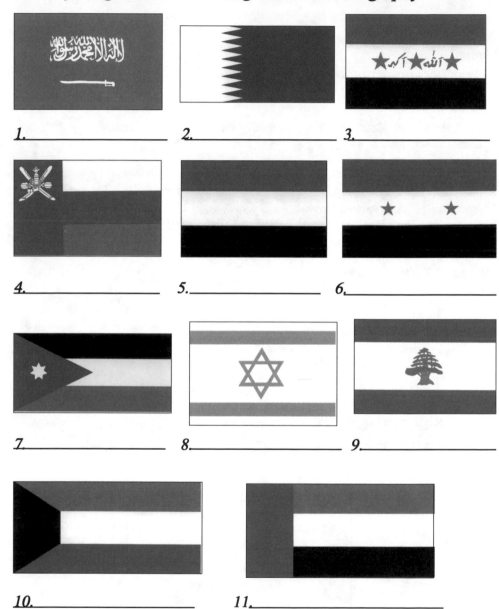

1._____

2._____

3._____

4._____

5._____

6._____

7._____

8._____

9._____

10._____

11._____

Identify Nations of Man Wearing Bow Tie Pictography.

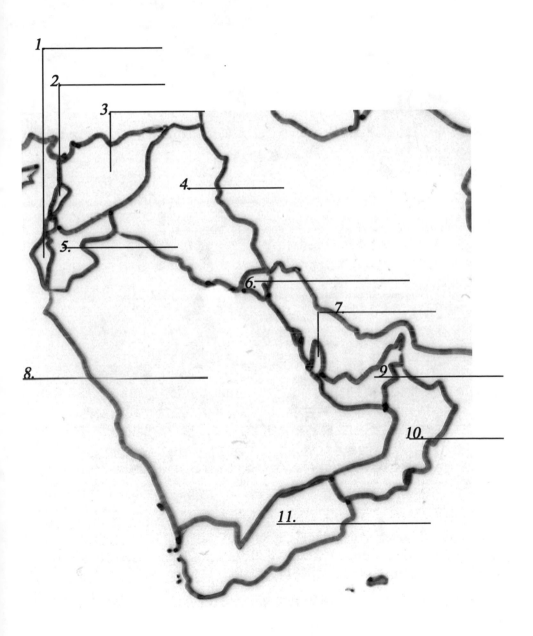

1.

2.

3.

4.

5.

6.

7.

8.

9.

10.

11.

<u>Oceania</u> *Scottie Dog*
Australia

Mnemonic Device: <u>Australia</u> is depicted as the <u>head of a Scottie</u>. Also, his <u>dog tag</u>, which is directly south of its head, is a part of Australia--the island of Tasmania.

Use Map and Fill in Facts.

Name of Nation_____
Capital_____
Boundaries (Bordering Nations and/or Bodies of Water):
1._____2._____3._____
   4._____5._____
   6._____7._____

Area: 2,967,896 sq. mi. **Comparative size:** slightly smaller than the USA contiguous 48 states

Terrain: mostly low plateau with deserts; fertile plain in southeast

Climate: generally arid to semiarid; temperate in south and east; tropical in north

Geographic Note: world's smallest continent but sixth-largest country; population concentrated along the eastern and southeastern coasts; regular, tropical sea breeze known as "the Doctor" occurs along the west coast in the summer

Population: 19,546,792 people

Languages: English, native languages

Religion: Anglican 26.1%, Catholic 26%, other Christian 24.3%, non-Christian 11%, other 12.6%

Type of Government: democratic, federal-state system recognizing the British monarch as sovereign

Exports: coal, gold, meat, wool, alumina, iron ore, wheat, machinery and transport equipment

Currency: Australian dollar (AUD)

FLAG DESCRIPTION: It has a blue field with the flag of the UK in the upper hoist-side quadrant. A large, seven-pointed star is in the lower, hoist-side quadrant. The remaining half is a representation of the Southern Cross constellation in white, with one small, five-pointed star, and four, larger, seven-pointed stars.

Draw and Color Flag.

Hoist   Fly

Mnemonic Device: <u>New</u> <u>Zealand</u> is depicted as the <u>collar</u> of the Scottie Pictography, which has, unfortunately, just fallen away.

Use Map and Fill in Facts.

Name of Nation_____

Capital_____

Boundaries (Bordering Nations and/or Bodies of Water):

    1._____2._____

Area: 103,737 sq. mi. **Comparative size:** about the size of Colorado

Terrain: predominately mountainous with some large coastal plains

Climate: temperate with sharp regional contrasts

Geographic Note: about 80% of the population lives in cities; Wellington is the southernmost national capital in the world

Population: 3,908,037 people

Languages: (official) English and Maori

Religion: Anglican 24%, Presbyterian 18%, Catholic 15%, Methodist 5%, Baptist 2%, other Protestant 3%, unspecified or none 33%

Type of Government: parliamentary democracy

Exports: dairy products, meat, wood and wood products, fish, machinery

Currency: New Zealand dollar (NZD)

FLAG DESCRIPTION: It has a blue field with the flag of the UK in the upper hoist-side quadrant. It has four red, five-pointed stars edged in white which are centered in the outer half of the flag. The stars represent the Southern Cross constellation.

Draw and Color Flag.

Hoist

Fly

Identify Flag's of Scottie Dog Pictography.

1._____   2._____

Identify Nation's of Scottie Dog Pictography.

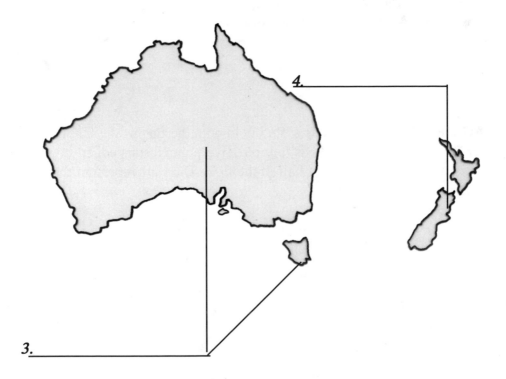

4._____

3._____

Europe *Boot*

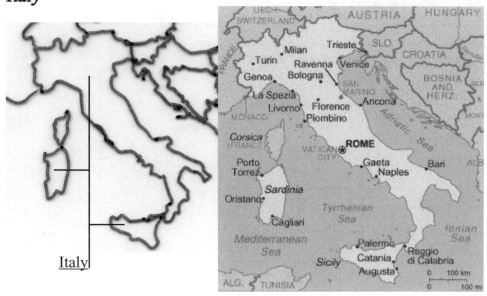

Italy

Mnemonic Device: People say that <u>Italy</u> looks like a <u>boot</u>. Go figure.

Use Map and Fill in Facts.

Name of Nation_____

Capital_____

Boundaries (Bordering Nations and/or Bodies of Water):

1._____ 2._____ 3._____

4._____ 5._____ 6._____

7._____ 8._____ 9._____

Area: 116,305 sq. mi. **Comparative size:** about the size of Arizona

Terrain: mostly rugged and mountainous; some plains coastal lowlands

Climate: Mediterranean; Alpine in far north; hot, dry in south

Geographic Note: strategic location dominating central Mediterranean as well as southern sea and air approaches to Western Europe

Population: 57,715,625 people

Languages: (official) Italian, German, French, Slovene

Religion: predominantly Roman Catholic with mature Protestant and Jewish communities; growing Muslim immigrant community

Type of Government: republic

Exports: engineering products, textiles and clothing, production machinery, motor vehicles, transport equipment, chemicals; food, beverages and tobacco; minerals and nonferrous metals

Currency: euro (EUR)

FLAG DESCRIPTION: There are three equal vertical bands: green (hoist side), white, and red. Inspired by the French flag brought to Italy by Napoleon in 1797.

Draw and Color Flag

Hoist

Fly

Europe

Boy Yelling, "Kick the Ball to Gary-a, Bulgaria"

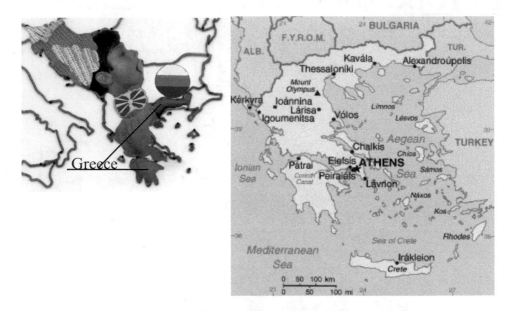

Mnemonic Device: The mainland of Greece is located in the southernmost part of the Balkan Peninsula. In the Ionian Sea and the Aegean Sea, there are more than 1,500 Greek Islands. Now this little boy is named Slavia. He is the best ball kicker on his team. His ball kicking success can be attributed to his discovery: putting <u>grease</u> on his foot, leg, and trousers, helps to glide the ball along. Hence, <u>Greece</u> is depicted as the <u>foot, leg, and trouser</u> of our Boy Yelling Pictography.

Use Map and Fill in Facts.

Name of Nation_____
Capital_____
Boundaries (Bordering Nations and/or Bodies of Water):
1._____ 2._____ 3._____
    4._____   5._____
    6._____   7._____

Area: 50,942 sq. mi. **Comparative size:** about the size of Alabama
Terrain: mostly mountains with ranges extending into the sea as peninsulas or chains of islands
Climate: temperate; mild, wet winters; hot, dry summers
Geographic Note: strategic location dominating the Aegean Sea and southern approach to Turkish Straits; a peninsular country, possessing an archipelago of about 2,000 islands
Population: 10,645,343 people
Languages: (official) Greek 99%; English, French
Religion: Greek Orthodox 98%; Muslim 1.3%, other 0.7%
Type of Government: parlimentary republic
Exports: food and beverages, manufactured goods, petroleum products, chemicals, textiles
Currency: euro (EUR)

FLAG DESCRIPTION: There are nine equal horizontal stripes of blue alternating with white. There is a blue square in the upper, hoist-side corner bearing a white cross. The cross symbolizes Greek Orthodoxy, the established religion of the country.

Draw and Color Flag.

Hoist   Fly

Serbia and Montenegro *(formally Yugoslavia)*

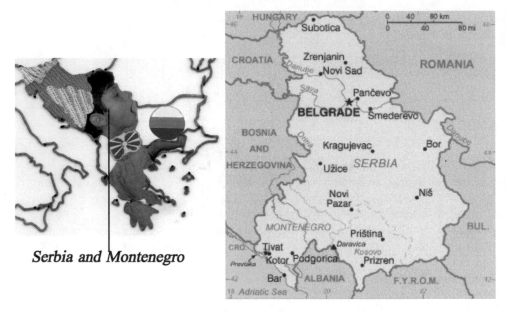

Serbia and Montenegro

Mnemonic Device: When Slavia (head, neck) plays against a rival team, all cheer him on by chanting: "you go Slavia, um hum, um hum...you go Slovia!" However, he has asked all who support his athletic efforts not to chant, you go Slavia anymore. He has decided to change his name to Serbia Montenegro. Perhaps he thinks it sounds more like a professional soccer player's name.

Use Map and Fill in Facts.

Name of Nation_____

Capital_____

Boundaries (Bordering Nations and/or Bodies of Water):

1._____ 2._____ 3._____

4._____ 5._____ 6._____

   7._____ 8._____

Area: 102,173 sq. mi. **Comparative size:** about the size of Kentucky

Terrain: north: rich fertile plains; east: limestone ranges and basins; southeast: mountains and hills; southwest: high shoreline with no islands off the coast

Climate: in the north, continental climate (cold winters, and hot, humid summers with well distributed rainfall); central portion, continental and Mediterranean climate; to the south, Adriatic climate along the coast: hot, dry summers, and autumns; cold winters with heavy snowfall inland

Geographic Note: controls one of the major land routes from Western Europe to Turkey and the Near East; strategic location along the Adriatic coast

Population: 10,656,929 people

Languages: Serbian 95%, Albanian 5%

Religion: Orthodox 65%, Muslim 19%, Catholic 4%, Protestant 1%, other 11%

Type of Government: republic

Exports: manufactured goods, food and live animals, raw materials

Currency: new Yugoslav dinar (YUM); note-in Montenegro the euro is legal tender; in Kosovo both the eruo and the Yugoslav dinar are legal

FLAG DESCRIPTION: There are three equal horizontal bands: blue (top), white, and red.

Draw and Color Flag.

Hoist

Fly

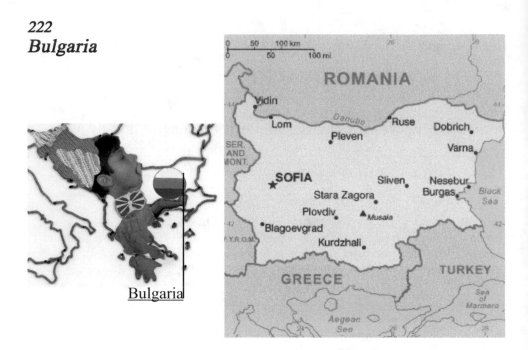

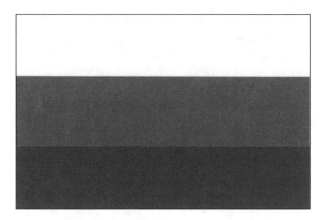

Bulgaria

Mnemonic Device: This boy kicks the ball farther than anyone in his league. While kicking the ball he yells, "kick the ball to Gary-a, <u>Bulgaria</u>." Gary-a is another star player on the team. The <u>ball</u> is shown within the borders of <u>Bulgaria</u> in our Boy Yelling Pictography.

Use Map and Fill in Facts.

Name of Nation_____
Capital_____
Boundaries (Bordering Nations and/or Bodies of Water):
1._____ 2._____ 3._____
4._____ 5._____ 6._____

Area: 42,823 sq. mi. **Comparative size:** about the size of Tennessee
Terrain: mostly mountains with lowlands in north and southeast
Climate: temperate; cold, damp winters; hot, dry summers
Geographic Note: strategic location near Turkish Straits; controls key land routes from Europe to Middle East and Asia
Population: 7,621,337 people
Languages: Bulgarian; secondary languages correspond to ethnic breakdown
Religion: Bulgarian Orthodox 83.8%, Muslim 12.1%, Catholic 1.7%, Jewish .1% Protestant, Gregorian-Armenian, and other 2.3%
Type of Government: parliamentary democracy
Exports: clothing, footwear, iron and steel, machinery and equipment, fuels
Currency: lev (BGL)

FLAG DESCRIPTION: There are three equal horizontal bands: white (top), green, and red.

Draw and Color Flag.

Hoist

Fly

Macedonia

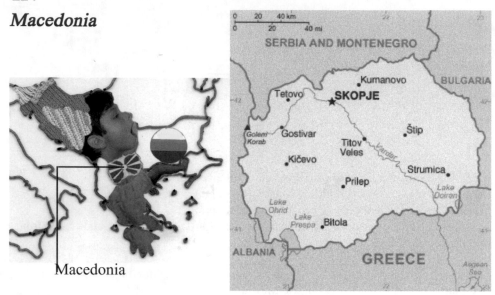

Macedonia

Mnemonic Device: This boy's team wears an unusual uniform. For example, the players are assigned a regulation bow tie that has the same colors and similar pattern as the flag of Macedonia. <u>Macedonia</u> is depicted as the <u>bow</u> <u>tie</u> of our Boy Yelling Pictography.

Use Map and Fill in Facts.

Name of Nation_____
Capital_____
Boundaries (Bordering Nations and/or Bodies of Water):
      1._____ 2._____
      3._____ 4._____

Area: 9,928 sq. mi. **Comparative size:** about the size of Vermont
Terrain: mountainous territory covered with deep basins and valleys; three large lakes, each divided by a frontier line; country bisected by Vardar River
Climate: warm, dry summers and autumns; relatively cold winters with heavy snowfall
Geographic Note: landlocked; major transportation corridor from Western and Central Europe to Aegean Sea and Southern Europe to Western Europe
Population: 2,054,800 people
Languages: Macedonian 70%, Albanian 21%, Turkish 3%, Serbo-Croatian 3%, other 3%
Religion: Macedonian Orthodox 67%, Muslim 30%, other 3%
Type of Government: emerging democracy
Exports: food, beverages, tobacco; miscellaneous manufactures, iron and steel
Currency: Macedonian denar (MKD)

FLAG DESCRIPTION: It has a rising sun with eight, yellow rays extending to the edges of the red field.

Draw and Color Flag

Hoist
Fly

Bosnia and Herzegovina

Bosnia and Herzegovina

Mnemonic Device: This boy is wearing his regulation, knit hat which is divided into three sections. The <u>lavender</u>, <u>triangular</u> <u>section</u> closest to the boy's head is <u>Bosnia and Herzegovina</u>. In a very low, "Papa-Bear" voice say, "Bosnia and Herzegovina". Note that if you invert the flag of Bosnia and Herzegovina, than the yellow triangle nestled within the navy blue field, resembles how this nation is nestled within the boundaries of Croatia.

Use Map and Fill in Facts.

Name of Nation_____
Capital_____
Boundaries (Bordering Nations and/or Bodies of Water):
      1._____2._____

Area: 19,741 sq. mi. **Comparative size:** about the size of West Virginia
Terrain: mountains and valleys
Climate: hot summers and cold winters; areas of high elevation have short, cool
summers and long severe winters; mild, rainy winters along coast
Geographic Note: within Bosnia and Herzegonvina's recognized borders, the country is
divided into a joint Bosniak/Croat Federation (about 51% of territory) and the Bosnian
Serb-led Republika, or RS (about 49% of territory)
Population: 3,964,388 people
Languages: Croatian, Serbian, Bosnian
Religion: Muslim 40%, Orthodox 31%, Catholic 15%, Protestant 4%, other 10%
Type of Government: emerging federal democratic republic
Exports: miscellaneous manufactures, crude materials
Currency: marka (BAM)

FLAG DESCRIPTION: It has a wide, medium blue, vertical band on the
fly side with a yellow, isosceles triangle abutting the band and the top of the
flag. The remainder of the flag is medium blue with seven full, five-
pointed, white stars and two, half stars on top and bottom along the hypot-
enuse of the triangle.

Draw and Color Flag.

Hoist   Fly

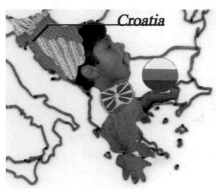

Mnemonic Device: <u>Croatia</u> is depicted as the <u>light blue, middle section of</u> the boy's <u>hat</u> in our Boy Yelling Pictography. Now in a rather medium, "Mama-bear" voice say, "Croatia".

Use Map and Fill in Facts.

Name of Nation_____

Capital_____

Boundaries (Bordering Nations and/or Bodies of Water):

1._____ 2._____ 3._____

4._____ 5._____

Area: 21,829 sq. mi. **Comparative size:** about the size of West Virginia

Terrain: flat plains along Hungarian border, low mountains and highlands near Adriatic coastline and islands

Climate: continental climate predominant with hot summers and cold winters; mild winters, dry summers along coast

Geographic Note: controls most land routes from Western Europe to Aegean Sea and Turkish Straits

Population: 4,390,751 people

Languages: Croatian 96%, other 4% (Italian, Hungarian, Czech, Slovak, German)

Religion: Catholic 76.5%, Orthodox 11.1%, Muslim 1.2%, Protestant 0.4% others and unknown 10.8%

Type of Government: presidential/parliamentary democracy

Exports: transport equipment, textiles, chemicals, foodstuffs, fuels

Currency: kuna (HRK)

FLAG DESCRIPTION: There are three equal horizontal bands: red (top), white, and blue. It has a Croatian coat of arms (red and white checkered).

Draw and Color Flag.

Hoist

Fly

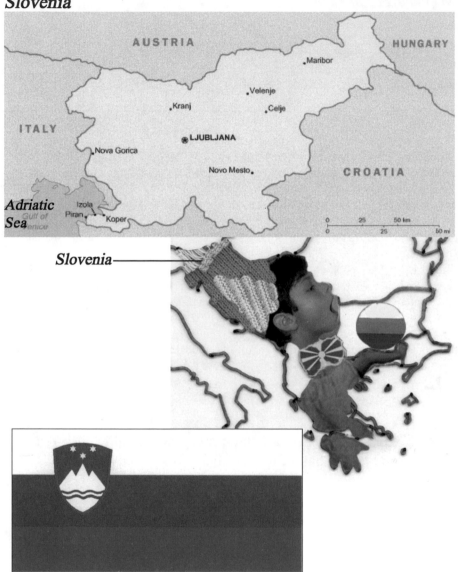

Mnemonic Device: <u>Slovenia</u> is depicted as the tassel on the tip top of the boy's knit hat on our Boy Yelling Pictography. Now in a teeny-weeny, "Baby-bear" voice say, "the <u>tip top</u> <u>tassel</u> is called <u>Slovenia</u>, and he wore it all up."

Use Map and Fill in Facts.

Name of Nation_____

Capital_____

Boundaries (Bordering Nations and/or Bodies of Water):

1._____ 2._____ 3._____

　　4._____ 5._____

Area: 7,819 sq. mi. **Comparative size:** slightly smaller than New Jersey
Terrain: a short coastal strip on the Adriatic, an alpine mountain region adjacent to
Italy and Austria, mixed mountain and valleys with numerous rivers to the east
Climate: Mediterranean climate on the coast, continental climate with mild to hot
summers and cold winters in the plateaus and valleys to the east
Geographic Note: despite its small size, this eastern Alpine country controls some of
Europe's major transit routes
Population: 1,932,917 people
Languages: Slovenian 91%, Serbo-Croatian 6%, other 3%
Religion: Catholic 70.8%, Lutheran 1%, Muslim 1%, atheist 4.3%, other 22.9%
Type of Government: presidential parliamentary democracy
Exports: manufactured goods, machinery and transport equipment, chemicals, food
Currency: tolar (SIT)

FLAG DESCRIPTION: There are three equal horizontal bands: white (top),
blue, and red, with the Slovenian seal (a shield with the image of Triglav,
Slovenia's highest peak, in white against a blue background at the center; beneath
it are two wavy blue lines depicting seas and rivers, and above it are three, six-
pointed stars arranged in an inverted triangle which are taken from the coat of
arms of the Counts of Celje, the great Slovene dynastic house of the late 14th and
early 15th centuries). The seal is located in the upper hoist side of the flag centered in the white and blue bands.

Draw and Color Flag.

Hoist　　　　　　　　　　　　　　　　　　　　Fly

Identify Flags of Boot and Boy Yelling Pictographies.

1._____

2._____

3._____

4._____

5._____

6._____

7._____

8._____

Identify Nations of Boot and Boy Yelling Pictographies.

1. _____

2. _____

3. _____

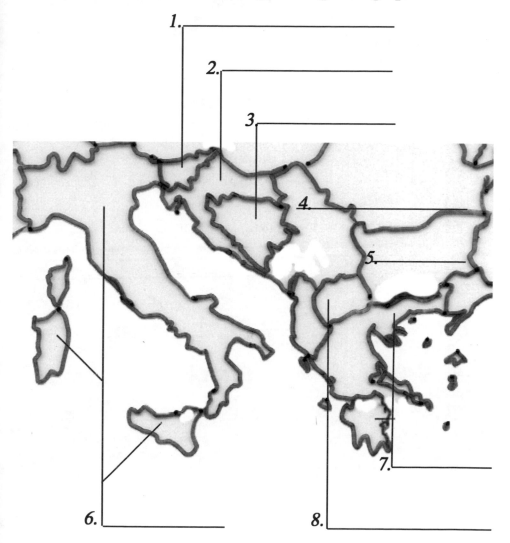

4. _____

5. _____

6. _____

7. _____

8. _____

Europe   *Hungry Elephant Wearing a Hat*

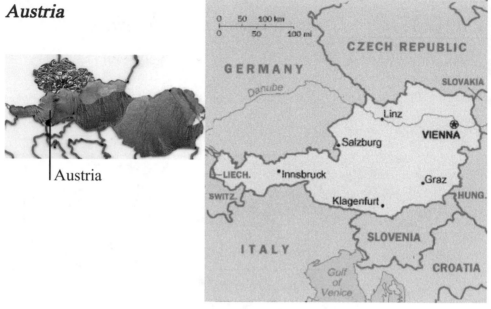

Austria

Mnemonic Device: Our European Elephant Pictography is about a very
hungry elephant who suffers with terrible allergies. His incessant sneezing
is such an issue for him that we refer to his face and trunk as
aw...aw...aw....STria. Hence, <u>Austria</u> is depicted as the <u>face and trunk</u> of
our European Elephant Pictography.

Use Map and Fill in Facts.

Name of Nation_____
Capital_____
Boundaries (Bordering Nations and/or Bodies of Water):
1._____ 2._____ 3._____
4._____ 5._____ 6._____
      7._____ 8._____

Area: 32,374 sq. mi. **Comparative size:** slightly smaller than Maine
Terrain: Alps mountains in the west and south; along the eastern and northern margins mostly flat
Climate: temperate; continental, cloudy; cold winters with frequent rain in lowlands
Geographic Note: landlocked; strategic location at the crossroads of central Europe with many easily traversable Alpine passes and valleys; major river is the Danube; population is concentrated on eastern lowlands because of steep slopes, poor soils, and low temperatures elsewhere
Population: 8,169,929 people
Languages: German
Religion: Catholic 78%, Protestant 5%, Muslim and other 17%
Type of Government: federal republic
Exports: machinery and equipment, motor vehicles and parts, paper and paperboard, metal goods, chemicals, iron and steel; textiles, foodstuffs
Currency: euro (EUR)

FLAG DESCRIPTION: There are three equal horizontal bands: red (top), white, and red.

Draw and Color Flag.

Hoist

Fly

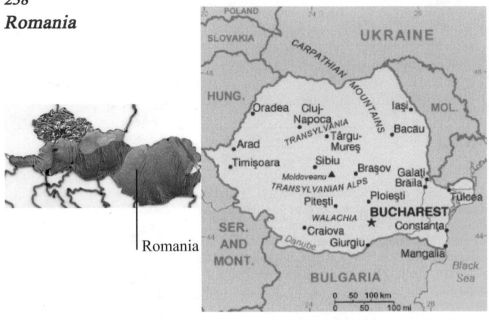

Romania

Mnemonic Device: Our allergy stricken elephant friend is often looking to eat. One day he decides that he wants to eat at a very elephant, I mean, elegant restaurant. His custom-sized car, however, is in the shop. So...he pulls out his row boat and places his <u>lower</u> <u>body</u> firmly therein. As he <u>rows</u> to the restaurant he sings, "Row, row, Romania, gently down the stream..." <u>Romania</u> is depicted as the <u>lower</u> <u>body</u> of our European Elephant Pictography.

Use Map and Fill in Facts.

Name of Nation_____
Capital_____
Boundaries (Bordering Nations and/or Bodies of Water):
1._____ 2._____ 3._____
4._____ 5._____ 6._____

Area: 91,700 sq. mi. **Comparative size:** slightly smaller than Oregon
Terrain: central Transylvanian Basin is separated from the Plain of Moldavia on the
east by the Carpathian Mountains and separated from the Walahian Plain on the south
by the Transylvanian Alps
Climate: temperate; cold, cloudy winters with frequent snow and fog; sunny summers
with frequent showers and thunderstorms
Geographic Note: controls most easily traversable land route between the Balkans,
Moldova, and Ukraine
Population: 22,317,730 people
Languages: Romanian, Hungarian, German
Religion: Eastern Orthodox (including all sub-denominations) 87%, Protestant 6.8%,
Catholic 5.6%, other (mostly Muslim) .4%, unaffiliated .2%
Type of Government: republic
Exports: textile and footwear 26%, metals and metal products 15%, machinery and
equipment 11%, minerals and fuels 6%
Currency: leu (ROL)

FLAG DESCRIPTION: There are three equal vertical bands: blue (hoist
side), yellow, and red. It looks like the flag of Chad.

Draw and Color Flag.

Hoist   Fly

Hungary

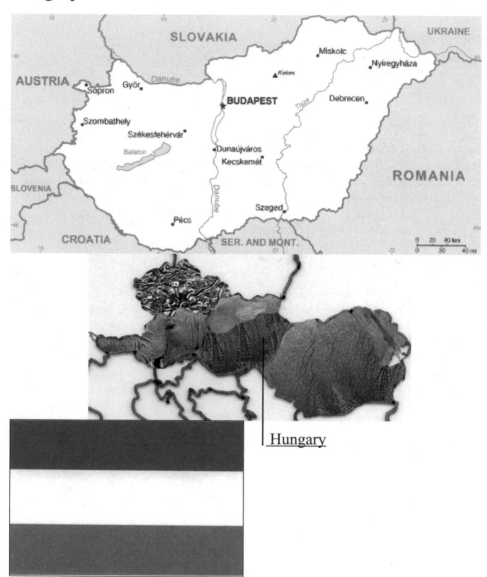

Hungary

Mnemonic Device: After rowing a short distance, our elephant friend is quite ravenous. Moreover, his sheer size, makes him always <u>hungry</u>, so that his stomach perpetually craves food! Hence, we refer to the <u>stomach</u> area of our European Elephant Pictography as <u>Hungary.</u>

Use Map and Fill in Facts.

Name of Nation_____
Capital_____
Boundaries (Bordering Nations and/or Bodies of Water):
1._____ 2._____ 3._____
4._____ 5._____ 6._____
                      7._____

Area: 35,919 sq. mi. **Comparative size:** slightly smaller than Indiana
Terrain: mostly flat to rolling plains; hills and low mountains on the Slovakian border
Climate: temperate; cold, cloudy, humid winters; warm summers
Geographic Note: landlocked; strategic location astride main land routes between Western Europe and Balkan Peninsula as well as between Ukraine and Mediterranean basin; the north-south flowing Duna (Danube) and Tisza Rivers divide the country into three large regions
Population: 10,075,034 people
Languages: Hungarian 98.2%, other 1.8%
Religion: Catholic 67.5%, Calvinist 20%, Lutheran 5%, atheist and other 7.5%
Type of Government: parliamentary democracy
Exports: machinery and equipment 59.5%, other manufactures 29.4%, food products 6.9%, raw materials 2.4%, fuels and electricity 1.8%
Currency: forint (HUF)

FLAG DESCRIPTION: There are three equal horizontal bands: red (top), white, and green.

Draw and Color Flag.

Hoist   Fly

Slovakia

Mnemonic Device: Upon arriving at the restaurant, the establishment immediately asks the elephant to check his hat. However, he is slow to hear their request since he is terribly preoccupied with feelings of insecurity. Is his rather enormous size going to preclude him from being seated? After the third time he is asked to check his hat, however, he is no longer slow to hear, and understands the correctness of it all. Hence, we refer to the ear of our Elephant Pictography as (Slow vakia) Slovakia.

Use the Map and Fill in Facts.

Name of Nation_____
Capital_____
Boundaries (Bordering Nations and/or Bodies of Water):
1._____ 2._____ 3._____
    4._____ 5._____

Area: 18,902 sq. mi. **Comparative size:** about twice the size of New Hampshire
Terrain: rugged mountains in the central and northern part and lowlands in the south
Climate: temperate; cool summers; cold, cloudy, humid winters
Geographic Note: landlocked; most of the country is rugged and mountainous; the
Tatra Mountains in the north are interspersed with many scenic lakes and valleys
Population: 5,422,366 people
Languages: (official) Slovak; Hungarian
Religion: Catholic 60.3%, atheist 9.7%, Protestant 8.4%, Orthodox 4.1%, and
other 17.5%
Type of Government: parliamentary democracy
Exports: machinery and transport equipment 39.4%, intermediate manufactured goods
27.5%, miscellaneous manufactured goods 13%, chemicals 8%
Currency: Slovak koruna (SKK)

FLAG DESCRIPTION: There are three equal horizontal bands: white
(top), blue, and red superimposed with the Slovak cross in a shield centered on the hoist side. The cross is white centered on a background of red
and blue.

Draw and Color Flag.

Hoist   Fly

Czech Republic

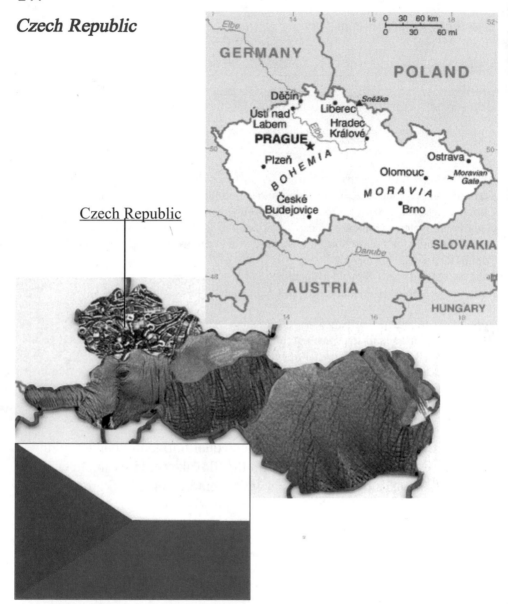

Czech Republic

Mnemonic Device: The elephant realizes that the request being made of him--to <u>check</u> his <u>hat</u>--is the right thing to do. He complies happily by re-moving his hat, and checking it at the door. Therefore, the elephant's <u>checked</u>, <u>gold</u> <u>hat</u>, depicts <u>Czech Republic</u>.

Use Map and Fill in Facts.

Name of Nation_____
Capital_____
Boundaries (Bordering Nations and/or Bodies of Water):
    1._____2._____
    3._____4._____

Area: 30,469 sq. mi. **Comparative size:** about the size South Carolina
Terrain: Bohemia in the west consists of rolling plains, hills, and plateaus surrounded by low mountains; Moravia in the east consists of very hilly country
Climate: temperate; cool summers; cold, cloudy, humid winters
Geographic Note: landlocked; strategically located astride some of oldest and most significant land routes in Europe; Moravian Gate is a traditional military corridor between the North European Plain and the Danube in central Europe
Population: 10,256,760 people
Languages: Czech
Religion: atheist 39.8%, Catholic 39.2%, Protestant 4.6%, Orthodox 3%, other 13.4%
Type of Government: parliamentary democracy
Exports: machinery and transport equipment 44%, intermediate manufactures 25%, chemicals 7%, raw materials and fuel 7%
Currency: Czech koruna (CZK)

FLAG DESCRIPTION: There are two equal horizontal bands: white (top), and red with a blue isosceles triangle based on the hoist side (same as the flag of the former Czechoslovalkia).

Draw and Color Flag.

      Hoist   Fly

Moldova

Mnemonic Device: Moldova is depicted as the <u>tail</u> <u>end</u> of our European Elephant Pictography.   It also happens to come at the end of our "Pictographies of the World" tour.

Use Map and Fill in Facts.

Name of Nation_____
Capital_____
Boundaries (Bordering Nations and/or Bodies of Water):
     1._____2._____

Area: 13,000 sq. mi. **Comparative size:** slightly larger than Maryland
Terrain: rolling steppe, gradual slope south to Black Sea
Climate: moderate winters, warm summers
Geographic Note: landlocked; well endowed with various sedimentary rocks and
minerals including sand, gravel, gypsum, and limestone
Population: 4,434,547 people
Languages: Moldovan (official, virtually the same as the Romanian language) and
Russian; Gagauz (a Turkish Dialect)
Religion: Eastern Orthodox 98%, Jewish 1.5%, Baptist and other .5%
Type of Government: republic
Exports: foodstuffs 42%, textiles and footwear, machinery
Currency: Moldovan leu (MDL)

FLAG DESCRIPTION: There are three equal vertical bands: blue (hoist side), yellow, and red. Centered in the yellow band is the emblem of a Roman eagle of gold, outlined in black with a red back and talons carrying a yellow cross in its beak and a green olive branch in its right talons and a yellow scepter in its left talons. On its breast is a shield divided horizontally (red over blue) with a stylized ox head, star, rose, and crescent all yellow, outlined in black.

Draw and Color Flag.

Hoist   Fly

Identify Flags of Hungry Elephant Wearing a Hat Pictography.

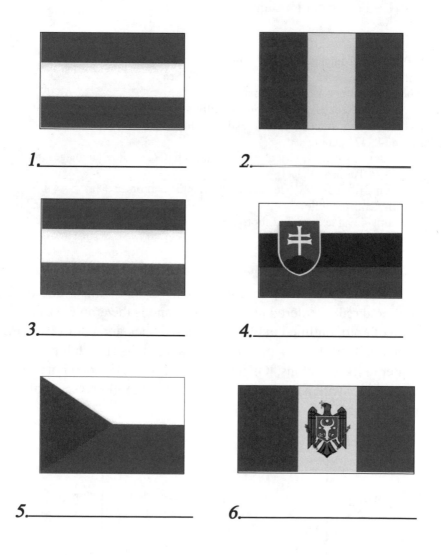

1._____   2._____

3._____   4._____

5._____   6._____

Identify Nations of Hungry Elephant Wearing a Hat Pictography.

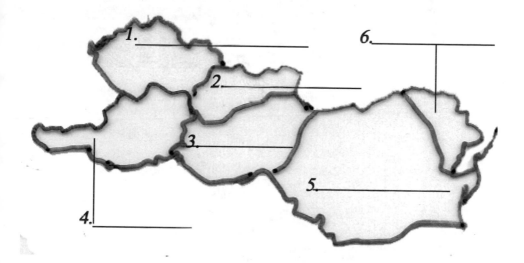

1. _____   6. _____

2. _____

3. _____

4. _____   5. _____

Note: Mnemonic Devices for the European Nations which follow will be in auditory form only: jingles on CD.

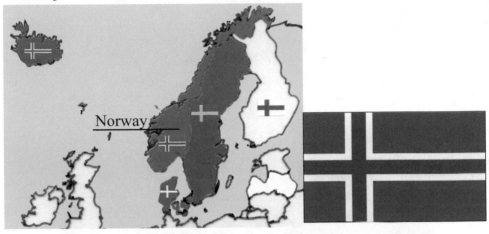

Use Map and Fill in Facts.

Name of Nation_____
Capital_____
Boundaries (Bordering Nations and/or Bodies of Water):
1._____ 2._____ 3._____
4._____ 5._____ 6._____

Area: 125,181 sq. mi. **Comparative size:** about the size of New Mexico
Terrain: glaciated; mostly high plateaus and rugged mountains broken by fertile valleys; small, scattered plains; coastline deeply indented by fiords; arctic tundra in north
Climate: temperate along coast; colder interior; rainy year-round on west coast
Geographic Note: about two-thirds mountains; some 50,000 islands off its much indented coastline; strategic location adjacent to sea lanes and air routes in North Atlantic; one of most rugged and longest coastlines in the world
Population: 4,523,116 people
Languages: (official) Norwegian; small Sami and Finnish-speaking minority
Religion: Evangelical Lutheran 86% (state church), other Protestant and Catholic 3%, other 1%, none and unknown 10%
Type of Government: constitutional monarchy
Exports: petroleum and petroleum products, machinery and equipment, metals, chemicals, ships, fish
Currency: Norwegian krone (NOK)

FLAG DESCRIPTION: It has a red field with a blue cross outlined in white that extends to the edges of the flag. The vertical part of the cross is shifted to the hoist side in the style of the Dannebrog (Danish flag).

Draw and Color Flag.

Hoist   Fly

Sweden

Use Map and Fill in Facts.

Name of Nation_____

Capital_____

Boundaries (Bordering Nations and/or Bodies of Water):

      1._____ 2._____

      3._____ 4._____

Area: 173,730 sq. mi. **Comparative size:** about the size of California

Terrain: mostly flat or gently rolling lowlands; mountains in west

Climate: temperate in south with cold, cloudy winters and cool, partly cloudy summers; subartic on north

Geographic Note: strategic location along Danish Straits linking Baltic and North Seas

Population: 8,876,744 people

Languages: Swedish; small Sami- and Finnish-speaking minorities

Religion: Lutheran 87%, Catholic, Orthodox, Baptist, Muslim, Jewish, Buddhist

Type of Government: constitutional monarchy

Exports: machinery 35%, motor vehicles, paper products, pulp and wood, iron and steel products, chemicals

Currency: Swedish krona (SEK)

FLAG DESCRIPTION: It has a blue field with a golden, yellow cross extending to the edges of the flag. The vertical part of the cross is shifted to the hoist side in the style of the Dannebrog (Danish flag).

Draw and Color Flag

Hoist   Fly

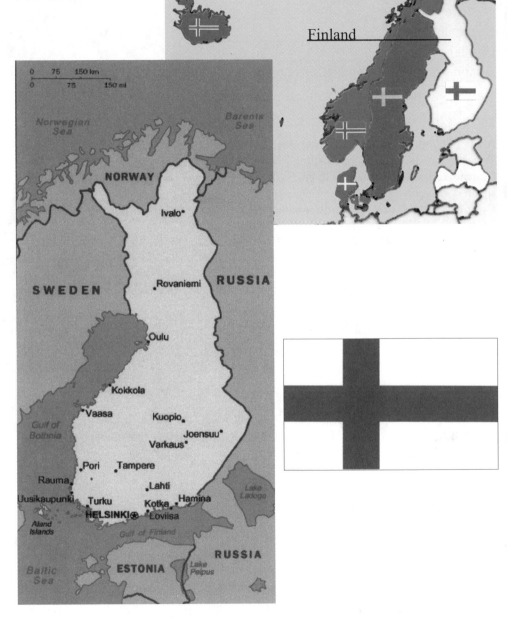

Use Map and Fill in Facts.

Name of Nation_____
Capital_____
Boundaries (Bordering Nations and/or Bodies of Water):
1._____ 2._____ 3._____
4._____ 5._____ 6._____

Area: 130,127 sq. mi. **Comparative size:** slightly smaller than Montana
Terrain: mostly low, flat to rolling plains interspersed with lakes and low hills
Climate: cold temperate; potentially subarctic; more than 60,000 lakes
Geographic Note: long boundary with Russia; Helsinki is northernmost national capital on European continent; population concentrated on small southwestern coastal plain
Population: 5,183,545 people
Languages: (official) Finnish 93.4% and Swedish 5.9%; small Lapp- and Russian-speaking minorities
Religion: Evangelical Lutheran 89%; Russian Orthodox 1%; none 9%; other 1%
Type of Government: republic
Exports: machinery and equipment, chemicals, metals; timber, paper, pulp
Currency: euro (EUR); markka (FIM)

FLAG DESCRIPTION: It has a white field with a blue cross extending to the edges of the flag. The vertical part of the cross is shifted to the hoist side in the style of the Dannebrog (Danish flag).

Draw and Color Flags

Hoist   Fly

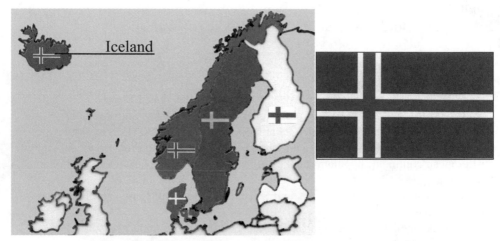

Iceland

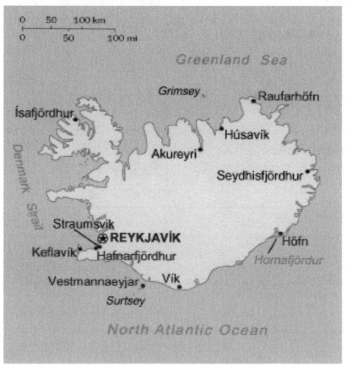

Use Map and Fill in Facts.

Name of Nation_____
Capital_____
Boundaries (Bordering Nations and/or Bodies of Water):
    1._____2._____

Area: 39,768 sq. mi. **Comparative size:** slightly smaller than Kentucky
Terrain: mostly plateau interspersed with mountain peaks, icefields; coast deeply indented by bays and fiords
Climate: temperate; mild, windy winters; damp, cool summers
Geographic Note: strategic location between Greenland and Europe; westernmost European country; Reykjavik is the northernmost national capital in the world; more land covered by glaciers than in all of continental Europe
Population: 279,384 people
Languages: Icelandic
Religion: Evangelical Lutheran 93%, other Protestant and Catholic, and none 7%
Type of Government: constitutional republic
Exports: fish and fish products 70%, animal products, aluminum, diatomite, ferrosilicon
Currency: Icelandic krona (ISK)

FLAG DESCRIPTION: It has a blue field with a red cross outlined in white extending to the edges of the flag. The vertical part of the cross is shifted to the hoist side in the style of the Dannebrog (Danish flag).

Draw and Color Flag.

Hoist

Fly

Denmark

Use Map and Fill in Facts.

Name of Nation_____
Capital_____
Boundaries (Bordering Nations and/or Bodies of Water):
1._____2._____3._____

Area: 16,629 sq. mi. **Comparative size:** about twice the size of Massachusetts
Terrain: low and flat to gently rolling plains
Climate: temperate; humid and overcast; mild, windy winters and cool summers
Geographic Note: controls Danish Straits (Skagerrak and Kattegat) linking Baltic and North Seas; about one-quarter of the population lives in greater Copenhagen
Population: 5,368,854 people
Languages: Danish, Faroese, Greenlandic (an Inuit dialect), German (small minority) note: English is the predominant second language
Religion: Evangelical Lutheran 95%, other Protestant and Catholic 3%, Muslim 2%
Type of Government: constitutional monarchy
Exports: machinery and instruments, meat and meat products, dairy products, fish, chemicals, furniture, ships, windmills
Currency: Danish krone (DKK)

FLAG DESCRIPTION: It has a red field with a white cross that extends to the edges of the flag. The vertical part of the cross is shifted to the hoist side, and that design element of the Dannenbrog (Danish flag) was subsequently adopted by the other Nordic countries of Finland, Iceland, Norway, and Sweden.

Draw and Color Flag.

Hoist   Fly

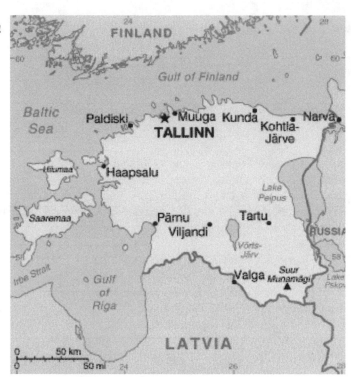

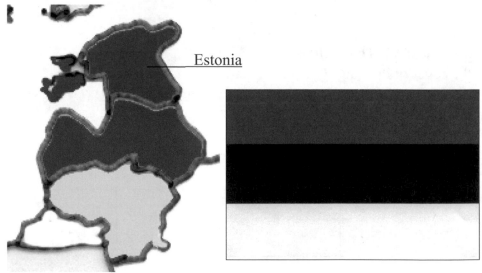

Estonia

Use Map and Fill in Facts.

Name of Nation_____
Capital_____
Boundaries (Bordering Nations and/or Bodies of Water):
    1._____ 2._____
    3._____ 4._____

Area: 17,400 sq. mi. **Comparative size:** about the size of New Hampshire and Vermont combined
Terrain: marshy, lowlands; flat in the north, hilly in the south
Climate: maritime; wet, moderate winters, cool summers
Geographic Note: the mainland terrain is flat, boggy, and partly wooded; offshore lie more than 1,500 islands
Population: 1,415,681 people
Languages: (official) Estonian; Russian, Ukrainian, Finnish, other
Religion: Evangelical Lutheran, Russian Orthodox, Estonian Orthodox, Baptist, Methodist, Seventh-Day Adventist, Catholic, Pentecostal, Word of Life, Jewish
Type of Government: parliamentary republic
Exports: machinery and equipment 33%, wood and paper 15%, textiles 14%, food products 8%, furniture 7%, metals, chemical products
Currency: Estonian kroon (EEK)

FLAG DESCRIPTION: There are three equal horizontal bands: blue (top), black, and white. Pre-1940 flag restored by Supreme Soviet in May 1990.

Draw and Color Flag.

Hoist

Fly

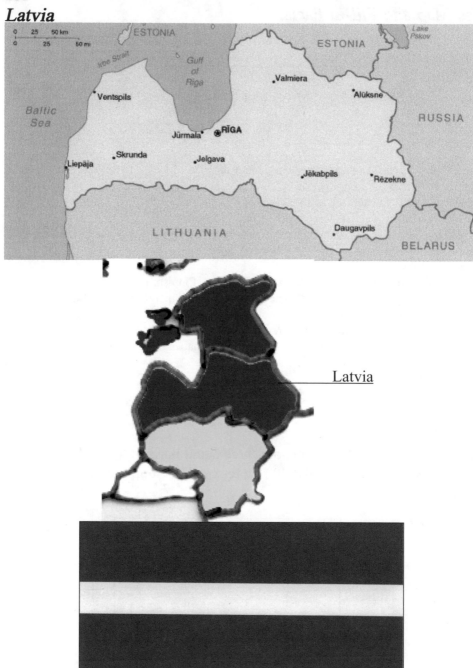

Latvia

Use Map and Fill in Facts.

Name of Nation_____
Capital_____
Boundaries (Bordering Nations and/or Bodies of Water):

    1._____2._____
3._____4._____5._____

Area: 24,900 sq. mi. **Comparative size:** slightly larger than West Virginia
Terrain: low plain
Climate: maritime; wet, moderate winters
Geographic Note: most the country is composed of fertile, low-lying plains
Population: 2,366,515 people
Languages: (official) Latvian; Lithuanian, Russian, other
Religion: Lutheran, Catholic, Russian Orthodox
Type of Government: parliamentary democracy
Exports: wood and wood products, machinery and equipment, metals, textiles, foodstuffs
Currency: Latvian lat (LVL)

FLAG DESCRIPTION: There are three horizontal bands: maroon (top), white (half-width), and maroon.

Draw and Color Flag.

Hoist

Fly

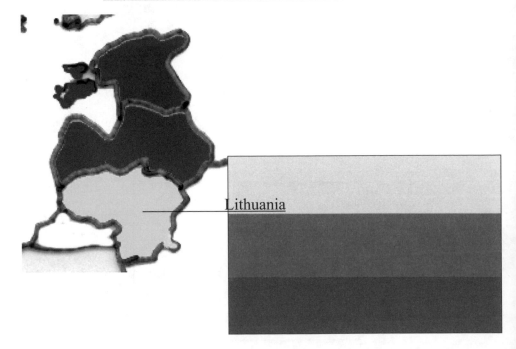

Lithuania

Use Map and Fill in Facts.

Name of Nation_____
Capital_____
Boundaries (Bordering Nations and/or Bodies of Water):
    1._____2._____
3._____4._____5._____

Area: 25,100 sq. mi. **Comparative size:** slightly larger than West Virginia
Terrain: lowland, many scattered small lakes, fertile soil
Climate: transitional, between maritime and continental; wet, moderate winters and summers
Geographic Note: fertile central plains are separated by hilly uplands that are ancient glacial deposits
Population: 3,601,138 people
Languages: (official) Lithuanian; Polish, Russian
Religion: Catholic (primarily), Lutheran, Russian Orthodox, Protestant, Evangelical Christian, Baptist, Muslim, Jewish
Type of Government: parliamentary democracy
Exports: mineral products 21%, textiles and clothing 19%, machinery and equipment 11%, chemicals 8%, wood and wood products 6%, foodstuffs 4%
Currency: litas (LTL)

FLAG DESCRIPTION: There are three equal horizontal bands: yellow (top), green, and red.

Draw and Color Flag.

Hoist   Fly

Identify Flags of These European Nations.

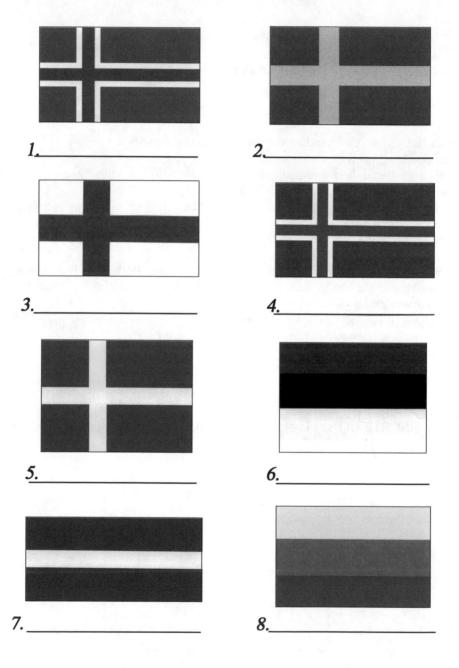

1._____

2._____

3._____

4._____

5._____

6._____

7._____

8._____

Identify These European Nations.

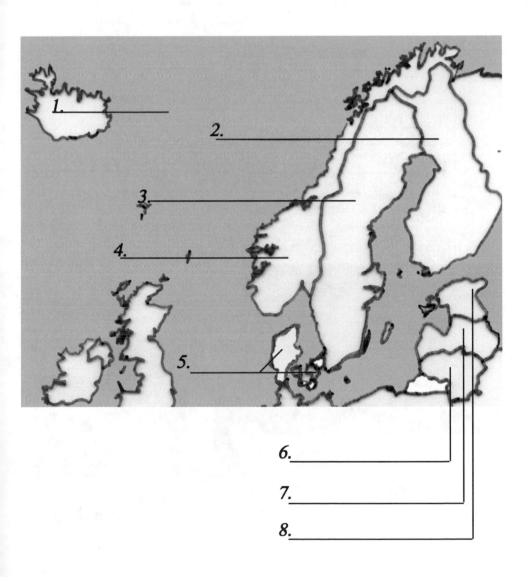

1. _____

2. _____

3. _____

4. _____

5. _____

6. _____

7. _____

8. _____

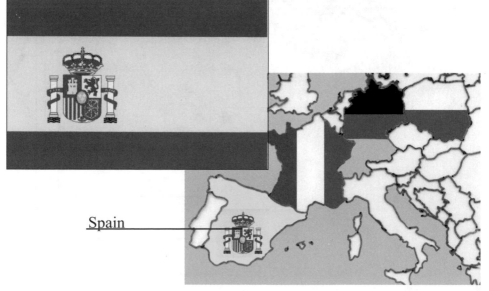

Spain

Use Map and Fill in Facts.

Name of Nation_____
Capital_____
Boundaries (Bordering Nations and/or Bodies of Water):
1._____2._____3._____
4._____5._____6._____
        7._____8._____
(***** Gult of Cadiz)
Area: 194,884 sq. mi. **Comparative size:** about twice the size of Oregon
Terrain: large, flat plateaus surrounded by rugged hills; Pyrenees in north
Climate: temperate; hot summers in interior, cloudy and cool along coast
Geographic Note: strategic location along approaches to Strait of Gilbraltar
Population: 40,077,100 people
Languages: (official) Castilian Spanish 74%; Catalan 17%, Galician 7%, Basque 2%
Religion: Catholic 94%, other 6%
Type of Government: parliamentary monarchy
Exports: machinery, motor vehicles; foodstuffs, other consumer goods
Currency: euro (EUR)

FLAG DESCRIPTION: There are three horizontal bands: red (top), yellow (double width), and red. The national coat of arms is on the hoist side of the yellow band. The coat of arms includes the royal seal framed by the Pillars of Hercules, which are the two promontories (Gibraltar and Ceuta) on either side of the eastern end of the Strait of Gibraltar.

Draw and Color Flag.

Hoist   Fly

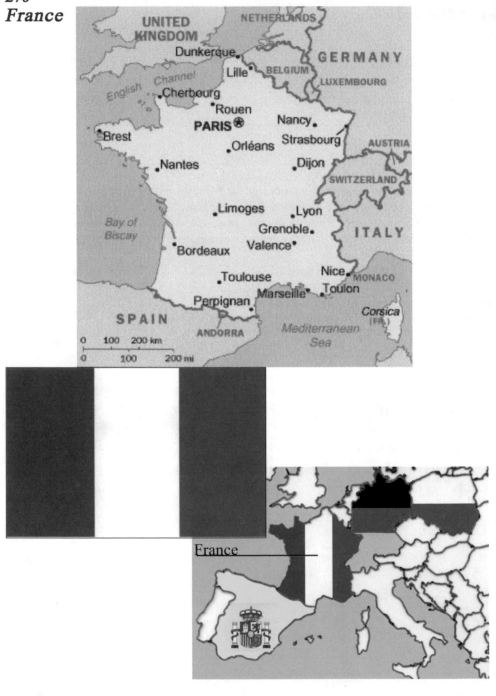

France

Use Map and Fill in Facts.

Name of Nation_____
Capital_____
Boundaries (Bordering Nations and/or Bodies of Water):
1._____ 2._____ 3._____
4._____ 5._____ 6._____
7._____ 8._____ 9._____
     10._____ 11._____

Area: 211,208 sq. mi. **Comparative size:** about twice the size of Colorado
Terrain: mostly flat plains or rolling hills in north and west; remainder is mountainous, especially Pyrenees in south, Alps in east
Climate: generally cool winters and mild summers; mild winters and hot summers along the Mediterranean
Geographic Note: largest West European nation
Population: 59,765,983 people
Languages: French 100%; rapidly declining regional dialects and languages (Provencal, Breton, Alsatian, Corsician, Catalan, Basque, Flemish)
Religion: Catholic 83-88%, Muslim 5-10%, Protestant 2%, Jewish 1%, unaffiliated 4%
Type of Government: republic
Exports: machinery and transportation equipment, aircraft, plastics, chemicals, pharmaceutical products, iron and steel, beverages
Currency: euro (EUR)
FLAG DESCRIPTION: There are three equal vertical bands: blue (hoist side), white, and red. It is known as the French Tricouleur (Tricolor).

Draw and Color Flag

Hoist   Fly

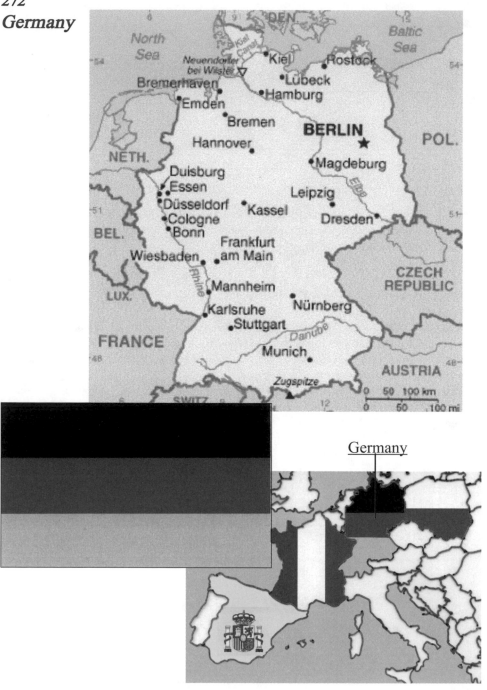

Germany

Use Map and Fill in Facts.

Name of Nation_____
Capital_____
Boundaries (Bordering Nations and/or Bodies of Water):
1._____ 2._____ 3._____
4._____ 5._____ 6._____
7._____ 8._____ 9._____
   10._____ 11._____

Area: 137,803 sq. mi. **Comparative size:** about the size of Montana
Terrain: lowland in north, uplands in center, Bavarian Alps in south
Climate: temperate and marine; cool, cloudy, wet winters and summers
Geographic Note: strategic location on North European Plain and along the entrance to the Baltic Sea
Population: 83,251,851 people
Languages: German
Religion: Protestant 34%, Catholic 34%, Muslim 3.7%, unaffiliated or other 28.3%
Type of Government: federal republic
Exports: machinery, vehicles, chemicals, metals and manufactures, foodstuffs, textiles
Currency: euro (EUR)

FLAG DESCRIPTION: There are three equal horizontal bands: black (top), red, and gold.

Draw and Color Flags.

Hoist   Fly

Poland

Use Map and Fill in Facts.

Name of Nation_____

Capital_____

Boundaries (Bordering Nations and/or Bodies of Water):

1._____ 2._____ 3._____
4._____ 5._____ 6._____
   7._____ 8._____

Area: 120,726 sq. mi. **Comparative size:** slightly larger than West Virginia
Terrain: mostly flat plain; mountains along southern border
Climate: temperate; severe winters with frequent precipitation; mild summers with frequent precipitation
Geographic Note: historically, an area of conflict because of flat terrain and the lack of natural barriers on the North European Plain
Population: 38,625,478 people
Languages: Polish
Religion: Catholic 95% (about 75% practicing), Eastern Orthodox, Protestant, other 5%
Type of Government: republic
Exports: machinery and transport equipment 30.2%, intermediate manufactured goods 25.5%, miscellaneous manufactured goods 20.9%, food and live animals 8.5%
Currency: zloty (PLN)

FLAG DESCRIPTION: There are two equal horizontal bands of white (top) and red.

Draw and Color Flag

Hoist

Fly

Identify Flags of These European Nations.

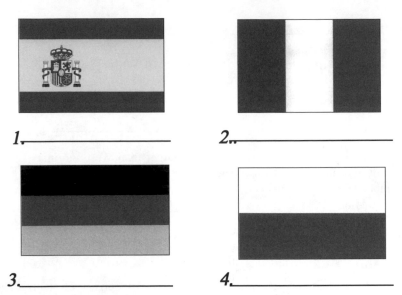

1._____

2._____

3._____

4._____

Identify These European Nations.

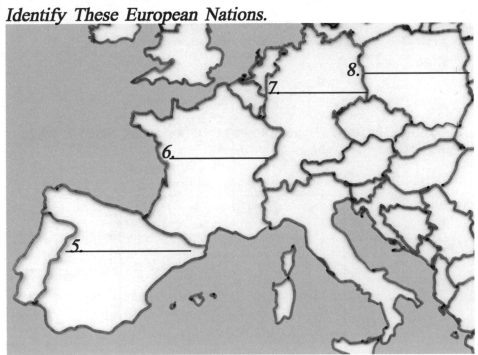

Russia

Area: 6,591,104 sq. mi. **Comparative size:** slightly less than 1.8 times the size of U.S.A.
Terrain: broad plain with low hills west of Urals; vast coniferous forest and tundra in Siberia; uplands and mountains along southern border regions
Climate: ranges from steppes in the south through humid continental in much of European Russia; subarctic in Siberia to tundra climate in the polar north; winters vary from cool along Black Sea coast to frigid in Siberia; summers vary from warm in the steppes to cool along Arctic coast
Geographic Note: in terms of area, it is the **largest country in the world**
Population: 144,978,573 people
Languages: Russian, over 100 other languages
Religion: Russian Orthodox, Muslim, other
Type of Government: federation
Exports: petroleum and petroleum products, natural gas, wood and wood products, metals, chemicals, and a wide variety of civilian and military manufactures
Currency: Russian ruble (RUR)

FLAG DESCRIPTION: Three equal horizontal bands of white (top), blue, and red.

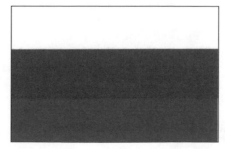

279

Answer Key

page 3: Burundi, Bujumbura; Rwanda
Tanzania, Lake Tanganyika, Demo. Rep. of
Congo

page 5: Djibouti, Djibouti; Ethiopia, Eritrea,
Red Sea, Gulf of Aden, Somalia

page 7: Egypt, Cairo; Mediterranean Sea,
Israel, Red Sea, Sudan, Libya

page 9: Eritrea, Asmara; Djibouti, Ethiopia,
Sudan, Red Sea

page 11: Ethiopia, Addis Ababa; Sudan,
Eritrea, Djibouti, Somalia, Kenya

page 13: Kenya, Nairobi; Ethiopia,
Somalia, Indian Ocean, Tanzania, Uganda,
Sudan

page 15: Rwanda, Kigali; Uganda,
Tanzania, Burundi, Demo. Rep. of Congo

page 17: Somalia, Mogadishu; Gulf of
Aden, Indian Ocean, Kenya, Ethiopia,
Djibouti

page 19: Sudan, Khartoum; Egypt, Red
Sea, Eritrea, Ethiopia, Kenya, Uganda, Demo.
Rep. of Congo, Central African Republic,
Chad, Libya

page 21: Tanzania, Dar Es Salaam;
Uganda, Kenya, Indian Ocean, Mozambique,
Malawi, Zambia, Demo. Rep. of Congo,
Burundi, Rwanda

page 23: Uganda, Kampala; Sudan, Kenya,
Lake Victoria, Tanzania, Rwanda, Demo.
Rep. of Congo

page 24: 1.Burundi 2.Djibouti 3.Egypt
4. Eritrea 5.Ethiopia 6.Kenya 7.Rwanda
8. Somalia 9. Sudan 10. Tanzania 11. Uganda

page 25: 1.Egypt 2.Sudan 3.Eritrea
4. Djibouti 5.Sudan 6.Uganda 7.Somalia
8.Rwanda 9.Kenya 10.Rwanda 11.Tanzania

page 29: Zambia, Lusaka; Tanzania, Demo.
Rep. of Congo, Malawi, Mozambique,
Zimbabwe, Botswana, Namibia, Angola

page 31: Malawi, Lilongwe; Tanzania,
Mozambique, Zambia

page 33: Angola, Luanda; Demo. Rep. of
Congo, Zambia, Namibia, Atlantic Ocean
(the Cabinda exclave is bounded by the
Congo, Demo. Rep. of Congo, and the
Atlantic Ocean)

page 34: 1. Zambia 2.Malawai 3.Angola
4. Angola 5.Zambia 6. Malawi

page 37: Mozambique, Maputo; Tanzania,
Indian Ocean, Mozambique Channel, South
Africa, Swaziland, Zimbabwe, Zambia,
Malawi

page 39: Zimbabwe, Harare; Mozambique,
South Africa, Botswana, Zambia

page 40: 1. Mozambique 2. Zimbabwe
3. Mozambique 4.Zimbabwe

page 43: Algeria, Algiers; Mediterranean
Sea, Tunisia, Libya, Niger, Mali, Mauritania,
Western Shara, Morocco

page 45: Morocco, Rabat; Strait of
Gibraltar, Mediterranean Sea, Algeria, Western
Sahara, Atlantic Ocean

page 47: Tunisia, Tunis; Mediterranean Sea, Libya, Algeria

page 49: Mali, Bamako; Algeria, Niger, Burkina Faso, Ivory Coast, Guinea, Senegal, Mauritania

page 51: Niger, Niamey; Algeria, Niger, Burkina Faso, Ivory Coast, Guinea, Senegal, Mauritania

page 53: Chad, N'Djamena; Libya, Sudan, Central African Republic, Cameroon, Nigeria, Niger

page 55: Central African Republic, Bangui; Chad, Sudan, Demo. Rep. of Congo; Congo, Cameroon

page 57: Democratic Republic of Congo, Kinshasa; Central African Republic, Sudan, Uganda, Rwanda, Burundi, Tanzania, Zambia, Angola, Congo

page 58: 1. Algeria 2.Morocco 3.Tunisia 4. Mali 5.Niger 6.Chad 7,Central African Republic 8. Democratic Republic of Congo

page 59: 1. Morocco 2.Tunisia 3.Algeria 4. Niger 5.Chad 6.Mali 7.Central African Republic 8. Democratic Republic of Congo

page 63: South Africa, Pretoria; Namibia, Botswana, Zimbabwe, Mozambique, Swaziland, Lesotho, Indian Ocean, Atlantic Ocean

page 65: Swaziland, Mbabane; Mozambique, South Africa

page 67: Lesotho, Maseru; South Africa

page 68: 1. South Africa 2. Swaziland 3. Lesotho 4.South Africa 5.Swaziland 6. Lesotho

page 71: Senegal, Dakar; Mauritania, Mali, Guinea, Guinea-Bissau, Gambia, Atlantic Ocean

page 73: Gambia, Banjul; Senegal, Atlantic Ocean

page 75: Guinea-Bissau, Bissau; Senegal, Guinea, Atlantic Ocean

page 77: Guinea, Conakry; Senegal, Mali, Cote D'Ivoire, Liberia, Sierra Leone, Atlantic Ocean, Guinea-Bissau

page 79: Sierra Leone, Freetown; Guinea, Liberia, Atlantic Ocean

page 81: Liberia, Monrovia; Sierra Leone, Guinea, Cote D'Ivoire, Atlantic Ocean

page 83: Cote D'Ivoire, Yamoussoukro; Liberia, Guinea, Mali, Burkina Faso, Ghana, Gulf of Guinea

page 85: Ghana, Accra; Cote D'Ivoire, Burkina Faso, Togo , Gulf of Guinea

page 87: Togo, Lome; Ghana, Benin Burkina Faso, Bight of Benin

page 89: Benin, Porto-Novo; Togo, Niger, Burkina Faso, Nigeria, Bight of Benin

page 91: Nigeria, Abuja; Benin, Niger, Chad, Cameroon, Gulf of Guinea page 92: 1. Senegal 2. Gambia 3.Guinea-Bissau 4. Guinea 5. Sierra Leone 6.Liberia 7. Cote D'Ivoire 8. Ghana 9. Togo 10. Benin 11. Nigeria

page 93: 1. Senegal 2. Gambia 3. Guinea-Bissau 4. .Liberia 5. Guinea 6. Sierra Leone 7. Ghana 8. Cote D'Ivoire 9. Togo 10 Benin 11. Nigeria

page 97: Venezuela, Caracas; Columbia, Brazil, Guyana, Caribbean Sea

page 99: Guyana, Georgetown; Venezuela, Brazil, Suriname, North Atlantic Ocean

page 100: 1. Venezuela 2. Guyana 3. Venezuela 4. Guyana

page 103: Chile, Santiago; South Pacific Ocean, Argentina, Bolivia, Peru

page 105: Argentina, Buenos Aires; South Atlantic Ocean, Uruguay, Paraguay, Bolivia, Chile, Brazil

page 107: Bolivia, La Paz; Peru, Brazil, Paraguay, Argentina, Chile

page 108: Argentina, Chile, Bolivia

page 111: Uruguay, Montevideo; Brazil, Argentina, South Atlantic Ocean

page 113: Paraguay, Asuncion; Brazil, Bolivia, Argentina

page 114: 1. Paraguay 2. Uruguay 3. Bolivia 4. Chile 5. Argentina 6. Paraguay 7. Uruguay

page 117: Peru, Lima; South Pacific Ocean, Bolivia, Brazil, Colombia, Ecuador, Chile

page 119: Ecuador, Quito; Colombia, Peru, Pacific Ocean

page 121: Colombia, Bogota; Venezuela, Brazil, Peru, Ecuador, North Pacific Ocean, Panama, Caribbearn Sea

page 122: 1. Peru 2. Ecuador 3. Colombia

page 123: 1. Columbia 2. Ecuador 3. Peru

page 125: Brazil, Brasilia; Atlantic Ocean, Uruguay, Argentina, Paraguay, Bolivia, Peru, Colombia, Venezuela, Guyana, Suriname, French Guiana

page 127: United States of America, Washington, D.C.; Atlantic Ocean, Mexico, Canada, Pacific Ocean, Gulf of Mexico

page 129: Canada, Ottawa; United States, Atlantic Ocean, Pacific Ocean, Artic Ocean

page 131: Mexico, Mexico City; Gulf of Mexico, United States, Caribbean Sea, Belize, Guatamala, Pacific Ocean

page 132: 1. United States 2. Canada 3. Mexico 4. United States 5. Canada 6. Mexico

page 135: Guatemala, Guatemala; Belize, Mexico, Pacific Ocean, El Salvador, Honduras, Caribbean Sea

page 137: El Salvador, San Salvador; North Pacific Ocean, Guatemala, Honduras page 139: Belize, Belmopan; Mexico, Guatemala, Caribbean Sea

page 141: Honduras, Tegucigalpa; Guatamala, El Salvador, North Pacific Ocean, Nicaragua, Caribbean Sea

page 143: Nicaragua, Managua; Honduras, North Pacific Ocean, Costa Rica, Caribbean Sea

page 145: Costa Rica San Jose; North Pacific Ocean, Panama, Caribbean Sea, Nicaragua

page 147: Panama, Panama; Costa Rica, Caribbean Sea, Colombia, North Pacific Ocean, Gulf of Panama

page 148: 1. Guatamala 2. El Salvador 3. Belize 4. Honduras 5. Nicaragua 6. Costa Rica 7. Panama

page 149: 1. Belize 2. Honduras 3. Nicaragua 4. El Salvador 5. Guatamala 6. Panama 7. Costa Rica

page 153: China, Beijing; Land: Mongolia, Russia, Kazakhstan, Kyrgyzstan, Tajikistan, North Korea, Hong Kong, Macau, Vietnam, Laos, Myanmar(Burma), India, Bhutan, Nepal, Pakistan, Afghanistan Water: Yellow Sea, East China Sea, South China Sea, Gulf of Tonkin

page 155: Thailand, Bangkok; Burma (Myanmar), Laos, Cambodia, Gulf of Thailand, Malaysia, Andaman Sea

page 157: North Korea, P'Yongyang; China, Sea of Japan, South Korea, Yellow Sea, Russia

page 159: South Korea, Seoul; Sea of Japan, North Korea, Yellow Sea

page 161: Malaysia, Kuala Lumpur; Brunei and Kalimantan, South China Sea, Indonesia, Singapore Strait, Singapore, Strait of Malacca, Thailand

page 163: Vietnam, Hanoi; China, Laos, Cambodia, Gulf of Tankin, South China Sea

page 165: Japan; Tokyo; La Perouse Strait, Pacific Ocean, Philippine Sea, East China Sea, Korea Strait, Sea of Japan

page 166: 1. China 2. Thailand 3. North Korea 4. South Korea 5. Malaysia 6. Vietnam 7. Japan

page 167: 1. Thailand 2. Malaysia 3.Vietnam, 4. China 5. North Korea 6. South Korea 7. Japan

page 169: Azerbaijan, Baku; Russia, Georgia, Iran, Caspian Sea, Armenia

page 171: Uzbekistan, Tashkent; Kazakhstan, Kyrgyzstan, Tajikistan, Turkmenistan, Afghanistan

page 172: 1. Azerbaijan 2. Uzbekistan 3. Azerbaijan 4. Uzbekistan

page 175: Nepal; Kathmandu; China India

page177: India, New Delhi; China, Nepal, Bhutan Myanmar (Burma), Bangladesh, Indian Ocean, Arabian Sea, Pakistan

284

page 269: Spain, Madrid; Bay of Biscay, France, Balearic Sea, Mediterranean Sea, Gibraltar, Gulf of Cadiz, Portugal, Atlantic Ocean

page 271: France, Paris; English Channel, Belgium, Luxembourg, Germany, Switzerland, Italy, Monaco, Mediterranean Sea, Spain, Andorra, Bay of Biscay

page 273: Germany, Berlin; Baltic Sea, Poland, Czech Republic, Austria, Switzerland, France, Luxembourg, Belgium, the Netherlands, North Sea, Denmark

page 275: Poland, Warsaw; Baltic Sea, Russia, Lithuania, Belarus, Ukraine, Slovakia, Czech Republic, Germany

page 276: 1. Spain 2. France 3. Germany 4. Poland 5. Spain 6. France 7. Germany 8. Poland

page 277: Borders of Russia: Norway Finland, Baltic Sea, Estonia, Latvia, Belarus, Sea of Azov, Ukraine, Black Sea, Georgia, Azerbaijan, Caspian Sea, Kazakhstan, China, Mongolia, North Korea, Sea of Japan, Sea of Okhotsk, Bering Sea, Arctic Ocean.

INDEX

CD Track Listing

Section I (Tracks 1-25). Pronunciation of Nations and Capitals for Older Listeners.

Track 1 & 26

Eagle on Rock: Burundi-Bujumbura, Djibouti-Djibouti, Egypt-Cairo, Eritrea-Asmara, Ethiopia-Addis Ababa, Kenya-Nairobi, Rwanda-Kijali, Somalia-Mogadishu, Sudan-Khartoum, Tanzania-Dar Es Salaam, Uganda-Kampala

Track 2 & 27

Boy in Bed: Zambia-Lusaka, Malawi-Lilongwe, Angola-Luada

Track 3& 28

Poodle and Ball: Mozambique-Maputo, Zimbabwe-Harare

Track 4 & 29

Al Cheery-A Clown: Algeria-Algiers, Morocco-Rabat, Tunisia-Tunis, Mali-Bamako, Niger-Niamey, Chad-N'Djamena, Central African Republic-Bangui, Democratic Republic of Congo-Kinshasa

Track 5 & 30

Hippo Wearing Shades: South Africa Pretoria (administrative); Cape Town (legislative); Bloemfontein (judicial), Swaziland-Mbabane, Lesotho-Maseru

Track 6 & 31

Snake: Senegal-Dakar, Gambia-Banjul, Guinea-Bissau-Bissau, Guinea-Conakry, Sierra Leone-Freetown, Liberia-Monrovia, Cote d'Ivoire-Yamoussoukro, Ghana-Accra, Togo-Lome, Benin-Porto-Novo, Nigeria-Abuja

Track 7 & 32

Elephant Named Ana: Venezuela-Caracas, Guyana-Georgetown

Track 8 & 33

Chili Pepper: Chile-Santiago, Argentina-Buenos Aires, Bolivia-La Paz

Track 9 & 34

"Guay" Game: Uruguay-Montevideo, Paraguay-Asuncion

Track 10 & 35

Jester: Peru-Lima, Ecuador-Quito, Columbia-Bogota
Brazil-Brasilia

Track 11 & 36

United States of America-Washington D.C., Canada-Ottawa, Mexico-Mexico City

Track 12 & 37
Man Eating Giant Ice Cream Cone: Guatemala-Guatemala, El Salvador-San Salvador, Belize-Belmopan, Honduras-Tegucigalpa, Nicaragua-Managua, Costa Rica-San Jose, Panama-Panama,

Track 13 & 38
Rooster Chasing Caterpillar: China-Beijing, Thailand-Bangkok, North Korea-P'yongyang, South Korea-Seoul, Malaysia-Kuala Lumpur, Vietnam-Hanoi, Japan-Tokyo

Track 14 & 39
Butterfly: Azerbiajan-Baku

Track 15 & 40
Arrow: Uzbekistan-Tashkent

Track 16 & 41
Ballerina: Nepal-Kathmandu, India-New Delhi

Track 17 & 42
Stan the Duck with Afghan: Pakistan-Islamabad, Afghanistan-Kabul

Track 18 & 43
Man Wearing Bow Tie: Saudi Arabia-Riyadh, Qatar-Doha, Iraq-Baghdad, United Arab Emirates-Abu Dhabi, Oman-Muscat, Yemen-Sanaa, Syria-Damascus, Jordan-Amman, Israel-Jerusalem, Lebanon-Beirut, Kuwait-Kuwait

Track 19 & 44
Scottie Dog: Australia-Canberra, New Zealand-Wellington

Track 20 & 45
Boot: Italy-Rome

Track 21 & 46
Boy Yelling, "Kick the Ball to Gary-a, Bulgaria": Greece-Athens, Serbia and Montenegro-Belgrade, Bulgaria-Sofia, Macedonia-Skopje, Bosnia and Herzegovina-Sarajevo, Croatia-Zagreb, Slovenia-Ljubljana

Track 22 & 47
Hungry Elephant Wearing a Hat: Austria-Vienna, Romania-Bucharest, Hungary-Budapest, Slovakia-Bratislava, Czech Republic-Prague, Moldova-Chisinau

Track 23 & 48
Norway-Oslo, Sweden-Stockholm, Finland-Helsinki, Iceland-Reykjavik, Denmark-Copenhagen

Track 24 & 49
Estonia-Tallinn, Latvia-Riga, Lithuania-Vilnius

Track 25 & 50
Spain-Madrid, France-Paris, Germany-Berlin, Poland-Warsaw, Russia-Moscow

Section II (Tracks 26-50). Pronunciation of Nations and Jingles for Younger Listeners.